PRAISE FOR C
MARKETING S

MW00582549

"Offers marketers a rich and much-needed understanding of content marketing."
Philip Kotler, S.C. Johnson & Son Distinguished Professor of International Marketing (emeritus), Kellogg School of Management, Northwestern University

"The frameworks and principles in Robert Rose's book are just what you need when it's time for a new strategy, a new project, a refresh of your annual plans, or welcoming new leadership to the mix. You'll be bookmarking and highlighting the heck out of this."
Jessica Bergmann, Vice President, Content and Customer Marketing, Salesforce

"If your goal is to build a strategic content marketing operation that grows in value over time, this book is your treasure map. You'll have to work hard, overcome obstacles, and dig deep to succeed, but this guide spells it all out clearly."
Joe McCambley, CMO, Saatva Luxury Mattresses

"Robert Rose's latest masterpiece truly provides the under the hood, nuts and bolts of how to execute superior content marketing strategy. This book is a much-needed deep dive on strategy—and the examples shared along the way are exceptional."
Amanda Todorovich, Executive Director, Digital Marketing, Cleveland Clinic

"Any organization looking to innovate and grow needs this as their modern marketing handbook."
Joe Pulizzi, author of *Epic Content Marketing* and *Content Inc.*

"Inconsistent goals and execution are the poison to successful content marketing. Robert Rose has given us the antidote. This is the ultimate roadmap for building—and more importantly, sustaining—a winning content approach that actually yields real-world business outcomes. Highly recommended!"
Jay Baer, author of *The Time to Win: How to Exceed Your Customers' Need for Speed*

"Robert Rose really does walk the content marketing talk. I am an avid marketing book reader, and I think I may not need another content marketing book."
Ian Truscott, Founder and SMO, Rockstar CMO

"This book takes the mystery out of what has become a buzzword in our industry, and makes it tangible to become a strategic advantage for today's contemporary marketers."
Marcus Collins, Marketing Professor, Ross School of Business, University of Michigan and bestselling author of *For The Culture*

"Content marketing has grown from a fuzzy experiment functioning in a corner of the building into a powerful, integrated discipline. This important book cements content's strategic role in every marketing department—including yours."
Ann Handley, *WSJ* bestselling author and Chief Content Officer, MarketingProfs

"I have rarely seen a better explanation of the word 'strategy', or a more hands-on guide to cultivating and managing a brand's content marketing efforts."
Bert Van Loon, Co-Founder, Content Marketing Fast Forward

Content Marketing Strategy

Harness the Power of Your Brand's Voice

Robert Rose

KoganPage

Publisher's note

Every possible effort has been made to ensure that the information contained in this book is accurate at the time of going to press, and the publishers and author cannot accept responsibility for any errors or omissions, however caused. No responsibility for loss or damage occasioned to any person acting, or refraining from action, as a result of the material in this publication can be accepted by the editor, the publisher or the author.

First published in Great Britain and the United States in 2023 by Kogan Page Limited

2nd Floor, 45 Gee Street
London
EC1V 3RS
United Kingdom

8 W 38th Street, Suite 902
New York, NY 10018
USA

4737/23 Ansari Road
Daryaganj
New Delhi 110002
India

www.koganpage.com

Kogan Page books are printed on paper from sustainable forests.

ISBNs

Hardback   978 1 3986 1152 8
Paperback 978 1 3986 1150 4
Ebook   978 1 3986 1151 1

British Library Cataloguing-in-Publication Data
A CIP record for this book is available from the British Library.

Library of Congress Cataloging-in-Publication Data
Names: Rose, Robert (Marketing executive), author.
Title: Content marketing strategy : harness the power of your
   brand's voice / Robert Rose.
Description: London ; New York, NY : Kogan Page, 2023. | Includes
   bibliographical references and index.
Identifiers: LCCN 2023024609 (print) | LCCN 2023024610 (ebook) | ISBN
   9781398611504 (paperback) | ISBN 9781398611528 (hardback) | ISBN
   9781398611511 (ebook)
Subjects: LCSH: Branding (Marketing) | Product management. |
   Marketing–Management.
Classification: LCC HF5415.1255 .R665 2023 (print) | LCC HF5415.1255
   (ebook) | DDC 658.8/27–dc23/eng/20230602
LC record available at https://lccn.loc.gov/2023024609
LC ebook record available at https://lccn.loc.gov/2023024610

Typeset by Integra Software Services, Pondicherry
Print production managed by Jellyfish
Printed and bound by CPI Group (UK) Ltd, Croydon, CR0 4YY

For my grandfather, Paul Rose, who used to say,

"Every experience you create is the opportunity to have impact on someone.
You choose—as well as get to experience yourself—what that impact will be."

My hope is that this book inspires you all to create your own remarkable experiences.

CONTENTS

FOREWORD

Welcome to the Fourth Media.

Robert Rose offers marketers a rich and much-needed understanding of content marketing. Most of a company's marketing is content marketing! Companies develop ads, brochures, websites, email, events, blogs, and other materials that carry messages and experiences. The content helps prospects and customers get hopefully a warm and trusting idea of a company. All the generated content should have good consistency and create a picture of a reliable and interesting company. Too often, however, the content seems miscellaneous and lacks consistency. There is no one person or team managing the content or developing needed new content. Rose, one of the most experienced content experts, invites the reader in to learn why the content of most companies fails to deliver full value.

Companies need to sort out how they contact, message, and relate to customers. Companies possess four broad media tools. The most familiar is *paid media*, where the company hires an agency to create ads and make sure these ads achieve sufficient reach and frequency. Then there is *social media* where a company sets up a position such as Facebook or Instagram, where they can be reached by and assist customers. A company can also use *earned media*, where their good deeds can be widely publicized through the assistance of public relations firms.

Now there is a fourth media, *owned media*, that a company can use to reach and influence customers and prospects. Owned media includes such company assets as a company magazine, blog, ordering platform, resource center, company podcasts, video series, and events. Yet companies tend to underuse their owned media and treat these marketing assets more casually. The company doesn't carry an account showing these marketing assets and their value. As a result, the company cannot show the CEO and company board members a return on owned assets or content.

Companies need to wake up to the value of these marketing assets. They need to get all their employees to know these assets and encourage them to use these assets and invent further assets. When the company finally appoints an owned assets responsibility person or group to manage and further these marketing assets, the company's performance and progress will be substantial.

Rose not only delivers everything we need to know about marketing content; his book also delivers valuable marketing insights. He recites the contributions of Peter Drucker, W. Edwards Deming, Theodore Levitt, Clayton Christensen, Don Schultz, and other notables. His book offers an excellent refresher course in modern marketing. His style of writing is cozy and personal and contains many stories of his extensive work with many companies seeking to incorporate content marketing.

Philip Kotler
S. C. Johnson & Son Distinguished Professor of International Marketing (emeritus), Kellogg School of Management, Northwestern University

ACKNOWLEDGMENTS

Benjamin Franklin once instructed "either write something worth reading or do something worth writing." In my case, if either of these things are true, it is only because of the remarkable people I have in my life.

First and foremost, if this book is in any way useful or practical, much of the credit goes to Cathy McKnight. She has been my co-conspirator in business consulting for more than a decade. She challenges my thinking, balances my weaknesses for details, greatly enhances any consulting skill I have at all, and, most importantly, laughs at my bad jokes.

The ongoing evolution of content marketing as a practice is due in large part to the extraordinary team at the Content Marketing Institute. Every single day I count myself blessed to work with such a talented group of friends. Their energy inspires me, their advice shapes me, they edit and shape my words, and they make me a better business storyteller every single day.

To Joe Pulizzi, my dear friend for more than 15 years, it is an honor to learn from you, laugh with you, and strategize with you. This book would not exist had it not been for our steak dinner in Chicago in 2008 when you convinced me to go "all in" on this new concept called content marketing.

There are also so many business leaders who I am proud to call friends. They open my mind, debate with me, and enable me to steal their insights as I integrate them into my work. I'm actually blessed to have too many to mention here. But if parts of this book have deeper levels of thinking, it is in part due to their inspiration. They include Dr. Tim Walters, Kim Moutsos, Michael Weiss, Jessica Bergmann, Ron Zwein, Steve Riley, Joe McCambley, Laura Barnes, Stephanie Stahl, and Dr. Marcus Collins.

I talk often of the value of doing the "quiet work", the work that doesn't call attention to itself. There are a few amazing people who have contributed to the quiet work of making this book worth reading. They include Brenda Newmann, who edited the first drafts of this book. She not only made it readable, but frequently saves me from my overly casual use of language. Thanks also to the wonderful team at Kogan Page who have made it easy, and a pleasure in managing the process of this book from idea to where it sits today.

Finally, I want to thank my family. Whatever success I've enjoyed throughout my career has been because of their magic, love, and unwavering belief in me. To Laura, for her uncanny ability to see through the mist of uncertainty and make the impossible seem so very possible. And to my wife of 30 years, Elizabeth, who every single day makes me feel that I, alone, am enough.

Introduction:
A New Old Story
Relearning a New But Familiar Practice

Marketing is telling the world you're a rock star. Content Marketing is showing the world you are one.

You're late.

But don't worry. I am too. I've been writing pieces of this book for the last seven years. But we're here, and as one of my mentors used to say to me, "As long as we're breathing, it's not too late."

So, take a breath.

Let's back up a moment. Hello. Welcome. I'm Robert Rose, and I've been working in the world of marketing and content strategy for nearly 30 years. I started as a marketing assistant in television at Showtime Networks in Los Angeles in 1995. It was, at that time, a "day gig" designed to pay the bills while I pursued a career in playwriting and screenwriting. However, it was there that I met some amazing people, who would turn me on to the art and science of marketing. It was a job that subsequently turned into a life's passion that still gets me out of bed every day. Throughout my career I've worked as a marketing research manager, product marketer, digital marketing consultant, director of sales and marketing, vice president of strategy, CMO, and back to consultant again. At every single step, my greatest joy has been rolling up my sleeves to do the real work of marketing and learning the myriad industries I've come to understand a bit better.

I am a student practitioner through and through. I proudly stand on the shoulders of the giants I've learned from, such as Peter Drucker, Michael Porter, Madam C.J. Walker, Theodore Levitt, Philip Kotler,

Don Schultz, Rita Gunther-McGrath, Youngme Moon, and Clayton Christensen. Whatever marketing thinking I bring to my clients, or my books, these are but a few of the teachers who helped me bring it forward.

What you're holding in your hand, or listening to, is the culmination of more than a decade of research, work, and personal experiences in deploying both successful and failed content-driven marketing strategies for businesses of all sizes.

Content marketing strategy lives

Wait, what? Content marketing *strategy*? Is that even a thing?

Yes. It is. Back in 2003, I was the CMO of a small startup technology company that focused on the (then) new and disruptive idea of enterprise cloud computing. As I like to say, we were in the cloud before being in the cloud was cool. There, I inadvertently helped create what would become more widely known as a content marketing approach. Our little company had no money, no brand, and little time to make a big dent in our market. We were, quite literally, working out of an old Victorian house with folding tables as desks.

Our competitors were the giants of the tech world, such as Microsoft, Hewlett-Packard (today's HP), and Oracle. They were selling traditional, server-based enterprise software while we were the disruptive new kid on the block. We knew we would never beat these companies when it came to SEO, advertising spend, event presence, or sales prowess. We were also emerging from the dot-com bust—so anything "new" or "innovative" was viewed with a healthy amount of skepticism.

So, as a ragtag team of business managers, we made a set of simple—yet at the time audacious—conclusions:

1 We knew we could be a mile deeper than any competitor when it came to subject matter expertise. We had a unique point of view about the future of enterprise marketing software (the idea that would become known as software-as-a-service) and we could help the world understand it better than anyone.

2 We all had media backgrounds—so we knew content and design. We knew how to create it, transform it, produce it, and distribute it, so we appeared much bigger and more impressive than we actually were.

We transformed our marketing team into a publishing unit. We used a substantial amount of our marketing budget to launch a blog, write white papers, create webinar programs, events, training. We became one of the few companies that reporters and analysts looked to for true guidance on where the software-as-a-service market was going.

Then, a funny thing happened. It worked. The company grew.

I found my calling. After a few years, I left the startup company in much more capable hands to grow into the successful company it would become, and I went all in on content marketing.

In 2009, I joined up with this guy named Joe Pulizzi who came from the world of business publishing. He had just formed a new media company called the Content Marketing Institute. I became their first chief strategy officer, and together we wrote one of the first books on content marketing strategy in 2011. We called it *Managing Content Marketing* because, at the time, we noticed the profound changes that digital technologies and social media were having on *both* the traditional worlds of publishing media and the practice of marketing. As we said back then:

> This new engagement of the consumer—with keen awareness of
> their relationships and emerging social networks—now correlates
> to every single aspect of our businesses. Marketing now influences
> how publishers publish, accountants account, researchers research,
> developers develop, service people service, and even how leaders
> lead.[1]

Our conclusion at the time was that yes, marketing and media have changed. The question is, what are we going to do about it?

The answer to that question was, of course, this new approach we called "content marketing." We wanted that book to be the "owner's manual" for how marketers could integrate this new effort into their ongoing marketing strategy.

An old, new story

So, here we are, a little more than a decade later (did I mention I feel late?), and content marketing strategy is still considered by many to be a new, innovative, and disruptive force. It's not that the approach hasn't grown in popularity or been covered by other authors. There have been hundreds of books on content marketing, covering everything from how to write more valuable content, to how to treat various digital content channels, to developing better customer relationships. Heck, even Joe and I, collectively, have written five other books on content marketing since 2011.

So, do we really need another book on content marketing? Why have *you* opened or tapped play on yet another book that claims it will enlighten you to the practice? Well, maybe the reason is because your business is still trying to figure out what content marketing is. Or perhaps you've tried content marketing and feel like it's not working for you the way you hear about it working for others. Or maybe you have a college professor who has assigned you this reading to understand this new process in business.

The reason I felt it was the right time is because so much of what is written about content marketing strategy focuses on either the first or the second word. I wanted to write what I've learned about the third word. Instead of writing a book about content, I wanted to write a book about how we *manage* content marketing. Strategically. So, yes, it's an old, new story.

But whatever your particular reason, maybe you feel late to the content marketing strategy party. So, here's something that will either comfort you or keep you up at night. Ready for it?

You are not alone.

Few companies have a content marketing strategy completely figured out. There are some that do, such as Cleveland Clinic, Red Bull, Arrow Electronics, HubSpot, and REI, that have purposely devised content marketing strategies that are meant to be differentiating. They have consciously designed, implemented, and measured a content marketing approach based on learned best practices. They are succeeding. But there are others, such as Amazon, Microsoft, JPMorgan Chase, and LEGO, that have backed into what *we* would call a smart content marketing strategy. They have built brand and marketing programs around the idea of developing valuable content and operating like a media company. However, most of these companies wouldn't consciously acknowledge that they built a content marketing strategy. If asked (and some of them have been), these companies would say that acquiring or launching a full media company operation was just a smart business strategy to diversify their ability to consistently reach their consumers. They're right, of course. They haven't read any of the books or been influenced by the Content Marketing Institute. They might not even recognize the fact that they're taking a unique approach to content marketing. And they are also succeeding.

As content marketing has grown as a practice, we've observed both types of companies over the years. You'll hear much more about both as we get deeper into this book. And, of course, content marketing isn't new at all. It, too, is an old, new story.

There has been no shortage of spilled digital ink talking about how content marketing has been around for at least 100 years. We all point to the Michelin Guide—a tire manufacturer that wrote a travel guide in the 1920s that evolved to become one of the premier global restaurant rating services. Yes, that's right—when you eat at a Michelin-starred restaurant the rating comes from the same company that makes the tires on your automobile. Or many will cite John Deere's *The Furrow* magazine and how, since 1895, this magazine has helped farmers understand how to farm better. Many will also look to LEGO as a prime historical example. This was a turnaround story, where the company utilized an ability to produce print magazines and feature films—and now digital experiences—to drive product stories. As the vice president of marketing there once said: "We used to be a toy manufacturer. Now we're turning more and more into a media company to tell our story about these bricks. We need a lot of content to tell that story."[2] These are all examples of companies that discovered the value of content marketing well before there was a name for it.

However, both these older companies and the new ones that have developed content marketing struggle with convincing their leadership that these initiatives are worth continuing. No matter how old the practice of content marketing, it remains a new concept for many businesses. Over the last few years I've met and/or consulted with every single one of the companies listed above, as well as many others that serve as "content marketing case studies" at conferences. The *people* in those companies, without exception, are just like all of us: They feel late, work hard, and lurch along an evolving journey to continue to make the business case. Every. Single. Day. The leader at one of the most frequently mentioned content marketing case studies said to me in 2022: "I wish my boss could see all the times we're mentioned as a case study for content marketing. I still fight for budget and relevance every single month."

So, guess what? The continuing struggle to create a business case for our creative approach of content marketing is not a sign that the practice is unproven, that the hundreds of books over the last decade were wrong, or that we should abandon hope for our past failed efforts. It's just a sign that content marketing is becoming a normal part of our beloved practice of marketing. Sometimes it works. Sometimes it doesn't. It is an art as much as a science, and marketers will always be in the business of balancing their relevance against broader business goals.

The biggest obstacle for content marketing now—and why I felt compelled to finish this book now—is that the classic content marketing adage "*we need to act like a media company*" is mostly misunderstood. What gets most companies into trouble is that they feel like content marketing is creating stuff that helps them market themselves as a media company would. Nope. It matters not whether your company understands content marketing as a discrete approach, or whether you're more like Amazon or Microsoft and just adopting a media operation model because it's smart business. The goal is not to *market* ourselves as a media company. The goal is for marketing to *operate* as a media company does. Our job is not to change content to fit a new marketing goal. The job is to change marketing to fit new content goals.

Content marketing is a new operation for which we build business cases—a scalable, functional model of content that's as important as any product or service we offer in our marketplace. When making a renewed business case for content marketing, remember that no single new marketing approach is going to change the business. However, one new approach to marketing can be a reason the business decides to change.

That's what this book is for. Change. Like I said, we're late. But neither of us is *too late*.

The world of marketing changed after 2020

Consider that, in 2019, my consulting firm helped 35 businesses develop a business case and strategy for content marketing as a function in the business. At least 25 of those focused on developing a better lead generation engine. Four focused on brand and purpose-driven strategies (things like climate, diversity, ESG, etc.). The one remaining business focused on loyalty and better customer experiences post-sale.

By the way, all these clients were firmly in the camp of "We're doing this project because we have to be more organized, measured, and scalable when it comes to valuable content."

Then, consider that, in 2022, we worked with 52 companies (yes, business has been good, thanks for noticing!). Thirty-nine of them were focused on how content marketing can help enhance every part of the business funnel. In other words, post-pandemic the question of content marketing was no longer one of how to enhance top-of-the-funnel marketing tactics. And it was no longer a question of how we can get more organized or measured around a branding strategy. The question was how to build a functional content and marketing *operation* strategy. Full stop.

Truth be told, this pronounced shift from focusing on content to the operation of content as a strategy is why this book is late. The business case and need now is this: How do we institute content marketing as a functional process, a key operation within the integrated marketing mix, and not just a series of well-produced content assets that are used in one-off campaigns?

The challenges that this book addresses are twofold:

1 How do you successfully build (or merge, as the case may be) marketing operations personnel who handle digital content strategy (governance, processes, structured content, data, and

technology) with content marketing team members (creating valuable, purpose-driven, delightful content experiences)?

2 How do you scale this new operation so that it is efficient, measurable, and manageable?

The evolved business case for content marketing has changed into building a strategic operation that can build value over time. This is your new objective. And you'd better be sharp about it because you're about to get yelled at (maybe you'll be yelling at yourself if you're a solopreneur).

If your 2023 business case for content marketing is to prove the concept by showing your boss how competitor X has an amazing blog, competitor Y won an award for their thought leadership program, or competitor Z is driving better brand awareness with their print magazine, you'll mostly get shrugged shoulders and a raised eyebrow. You see, many marketers are still answering the "Why should we do content marketing?" question with "More, great, content." They wonder why the C-suite would be skeptical. But the truth is they aren't. They're wondering why it's taken so long for us to get to more, great, content. "You're late!" Put simply: Many content marketers are asking to build this new innovative media product and the CEO is saying, "We're not even good at what we're already doing, and yet you want to build something new?"

What content marketing strategy is about

Make no bones about it—this pushback from the C-suite hits every aspect of any content marketing strategy we want to implement. As an example, consider two very different companies—one a B2C retail company and the other a B2B technology consulting firm. In both cases, the company's CEO issued a directive to launch strategic content marketing as a core piece of their communications strategy. But here's the thing: Neither of those CEOs said the words "content marketing strategy." Rather, the directive from one was to get a strategy rolling to become the most recognized thought leader in their space. The other's mandate was to find a way to reach new audiences with digital media versions of their valuable products.

Both CEOs also challenged their teams to handle these initiatives without increasing their budgets. Rather, they said, "Find a way to do it with all the content you're already producing."

Both companies had to fix the entirety of content as a strategic function in order to make the resources available to accomplish their very different objectives. "Beware," one of them said to us. "Our CEO now doesn't believe we can do this. She believes we already have too much content." But, as it turned out, it was not that the CEO didn't believe in content marketing. Nor was it that she didn't understand what content marketing is. She simply questioned why no one had bothered to think strategically about how to operationalize all this stuff in the first place.

That's what this book addresses—a modern way to think about evolving a content marketing strategy.

Four challenges to inspire this book

In my continuing role as chief strategy advisor for the Content Marketing Institute (CMI), I've been lucky enough to help plan and study the organization's global research efforts for the last 11 years. In CMI's 2023 research across thousands of marketers at businesses large and small, we examined which factors marketers attributed to having little or no content marketing success.

By a huge margin, the top two factors were "content creation challenges" and "strategy issues."

To the point I made earlier, this is where the *"we-already-suck-at-it"* pushback originates. Senior management are quite right in asking why they should invest *more* in content, when the brand struggles to manage and measure the content you're already creating.

Of course, most businesses are far too genteel for anyone to say this part out loud. In modern business, senior management couch their concerns with responses like:

- "There is already too much content. Shouldn't we reduce the amount of content we are creating?"

- "Content marketing costs too much. Isn't social/search advertising/ paid media more efficient?"

- "How can we compete? I don't know if we're capable of creating differentiated content. Isn't there too much noise these days?"
- "We can't tie the content marketing approach to revenue. Where's the data? How will we measure this?"

Let's first acknowledge that every single one of these concerns is or has been true at different times. In this book, we'll look at the modern business case for content marketing and put it in the context of where we are today. We'll also explore frameworks for looking at each of these concerns.

Concern 1: There's already too much content

Here's an interesting twist that we've found across the hundreds of clients we've worked with over the last couple of years. Almost none of them create too much content. Yup, you read that right—almost none of them. But almost all of them create too many assets.

Wait, what? What do we mean by that?

As marketers and business practitioners, we are trained to think container first, content second. We start with "I need a web page" or "I need an email" or "I need a blog post." Then we go right to creating content for that container. It's inefficient and it assumes that ideas are cheap and the value of content is realized in the production and design (as opposed to content creation) capabilities.

This focus on content production is a symptom of not having codified any type of strategic content operating model. Yes, we can build a smart "factory" of content, but unless there's a specific purpose behind what we put on the assembly line, the widgets won't ever be valuable, no matter how glittery the design, and we won't know when we're making too many.

This book will explore an answer to the "there's already too much content" objection. We'll acknowledge it and respond that this is the primary business opportunity for putting a strategy behind content marketing.

Developing an operational model for content marketing is the critical piece of solving your ability to track how much you are spending *and* to plan, activate, and measure all the content you will produce.

That brings us to the second concern we'll address in this book.

Concern 2: Content marketing costs more

Somewhere in the collective consciousness of marketing—especially digital marketing—"paid media" (e.g., advertising) became the de facto standard for how much things should cost. Any new approach to marketing that comes along is put through the same filter. Is it cheaper or more expensive than advertising? If it's cheaper, it must be worth doing, and if it's more expensive, it's not.

The troubling thing about this question is that it makes two assumptions: (1) "Advertising" and the costs associated with it are as good as it's going to get and won't degrade further; and (2) we are pitching content marketing as a replacement for paid media (spoiler alert: This is the biggest culprit for the business case challenge). In other words, it may be true that content marketing is more expensive than advertising today, but what if advertising completely fails one day and we haven't invested in an alternative form of marketing? Or what if (and hear me out just a second) advertising on its own actually costs more than we truly admit?

That brings us to the second (and bigger) erroneous assumption—that we are proposing content marketing as a replacement for advertising. This isn't true. Content marketing provides multiple ways to draw value and ALL of them are interdependent with public relations, paid media, sales, and even loyalty programs.

At its heart, a great content marketing program is a media *product* operation that builds, activates, and promotes our customer experiences and ultimately benefits the sale of our other products and services. In this book, I will present a framework that demonstrates the role content marketing plays in the marketing mix. Content marketing should not be implemented as a set of one-off campaigns that are meant to replace (or be cheaper than) paid media advertisements. In fact, quite the opposite: The content marketing approach is about developing the *product of content*, with which we will integrate all other types of marketing, including paid media.

Concern 3: Our brand can't compete with content marketing

If our business were hurting, and the head of product management came to the CEO and said, "We can't create great products," how might the CEO react?

What if that situation were reversed? In either case, the head of product management might be looking for a job. The ability to create great products and services is *core* to a business.

If we're treating content seriously, why would we expect anything less? The only reason this assertion will be true is if we don't try hard or care.

Remember, exceedingly few companies have this truly figured out. You are *not* too late. Not yet. As an example, PR firm Edelman and LinkedIn recently conducted research about the potential of thought leadership for B2B marketing. Almost half (48 percent) of decision-makers spend an hour or more per week engaged in thought leadership.[3] Then, 15 percent of those same decision-makers rated the quality of the thought leadership as "excellent."[4] Further, only 29 percent of them said they gain valuable insights more than half the time.[5]

If you're not providing the best content for your industry, the real question is, who is? Are you going to rely on your competitors to set the bar (or fail to, as the case may be) for what "smart" or "valuable" looks like in your business? Every successful business these days has a way of demonstrating differentiating value through the way it communicates. Everything else can be copied.

This book will demystify the business storytelling process and provide a framework for how marketing practitioners can start to think about getting to a differentiating core story.

That brings us to the last objection that we'll cover in this book.

Concern 4: We can't tie content marketing to revenue

The short answer here is: Then don't.

There are myriad other ways to associate content marketing with adding wealth to the business. Revenue is but one.

We can dig deeper. The real assertion here, however, is that content marketing is "too fuzzy" to associate with a sale—and thus it's hard to draw a straight line to revenue. Now, this may be true, but it's not an argument for not doing content marketing. This is simply a challenge to how you design your measurement program—and to ensuring you apply the proper goals to your content marketing operation. Show me a company that struggles to measure content marketing, and I'll show you a company that struggles to measure marketing.

Each of the various content operating models will have different (and distinct) measurement goals. This is why it's so critical to understand the operating model. In this book, we'll examine how to design a measurement plan that is actually rooted in business value for content marketing and demonstrates value as a long-term investment.

This is what we're really striving for: a business case for a content operating model that drives value for the entire business.

This book is a question, not an answer

Most business books are meant to provide degrees of clarity around what's on the horizon. As I write the introduction to this book in December 2022, I'm sitting on a deck here in Santa Barbara, California, overlooking the beach, and it's a gray, rainy day. My view is varied shades of gray; the sand, the water, the sky, all different, and yet so similar that they seem to merge with one another. I can't help but appreciate the metaphor.

If I've learned any one thing in working on content marketing strategy for the last two decades, it's that there is no such thing as perfect clarity, or the perfect content marketing strategy. It's all shades of gray.

I won't promise you that this book will give you a paint-by-numbers checklist to create a strategy that's guaranteed for your business. Some of the models will be right for you. Some of the models will be wrong. Hopefully, all of them will be useful in some way.

Here's what I know. The strongest content marketing strategies I've ever seen are all built to do one thing: change.

Marketing is evolving. Yes. Again. But interestingly, and perhaps in a way ironically, both content strategy and marketing as practices are becoming more valuable and more enriching to the business. How?

Well, let me just pose this as the first question. What if content and marketing in the future (as practices) and their output were treated just as importantly in your business as the development of your current products or services? In other words, what if, in the future, marketing was seen not just as an expense line item in business that is made up of activities that use content to *describe the value* of your products and services so that you might reach audiences and persuade them to become customers? What if, rather, marketing was seen as a profit center where the primary function is to *create valuable experiential media-driven products* for audiences that can be monetized in multiple ways—one of which is the expanded or ongoing purchase of your traditional products and services?

Now, some of you (only a few, to be sure) are saying, "Hey, wait a minute, Robert. Didn't you also write a book about this very thing called *Killing Marketing*?"

Well, yes and no.

In our 2017 book, Joe and I argued a business case for content marketing, saying that it might become one way that a business can start to create marketing programs that also pay for themselves. We said that the practice of content marketing might eventually blend into the overall marketing strategy approach.

As I sit here and watch the rain on the beach, and the grays merging with one another, I can't help but think of the possibility that it might actually be the other way around.

It might be that the entire practice of marketing will morph into what we now call content marketing.

What if we content marketers and our approach to adding value, monetizing audiences, and treating all of our content as being as important as a product are the future of marketing, full stop?

There's a famous quote attributed to Peter Drucker: "The best way to predict the future is to create it." Whether or not he said it, there is a variant that I prefer. Dennis Gabor, a physicist who won the Nobel Prize, wrote a book called *Inventing the Future*. In it, he says a version of the quote that I like better in a modern world of technology and artificial intelligence:

> Rational thinking, even assisted by any conceivable electronic computers cannot predict the future... All it can do is map out the probability... Technological and social inventions are broadening this probability all the time... The future cannot be predicted, but futures can be invented.[6]

In the pages ahead I've got a few more questions for you to ponder. It's time to start inventing futures. I can think of no more perfect person to do that than you.

It's your story. Tell it well.

Notes

1 Pulizzi, J., Rose, R., and Hayzlett, J. (2011) *Managing Content Marketing: The real-world guide for creating passionate subscribers to your brand*, Cleveland, OH: McGraw-Hill Education, p.7

2 Millington, A. (2015) Lego says it wants to be a "small giant" as it backs consumer-focused marketing, *Marketing Week*, www.marketingweek.com/lego-says-it-wants-to-be-a-small-giant-with-consumer-focused-marketing/ (archived at https://perma.cc/HJS5-4HM7)

3 Kingbury, J., Bernoff, D., Barik, T., and Buzicky, H. (2021) Thought Leadership Impact Study, LinkedIn & Edelman, https://business.linkedin.com/marketing-solutions/b2b-thought-leadership-research (archived at https://perma.cc/6W3G-VGPJ)

4 Ibid

5 Ibid

6 Gabor, D. (1972) *Inventing the Future*, Harmondsworth: Penguin Books, p.207

Content, Marketing, and Strategy

Maximizing Marketing's Potential

Your content will never provide competitive advantage. But your content strategy just might.

Let's begin with a secret. Are you ready?

The content you create provides no sustainable competitive advantage.

That's one heck of a way to start a book about why content marketing strategy will ultimately benefit your business. But it bears repeating. None of the content you create will provide your brand any kind of sustainable competitive advantage.

Most businesses don't understand this. And it is why they fail to create either a successful marketing or content strategy.

In 2005, author David Foster Wallace addressed the graduating class at Kenyon College with a speech that would become one of his most-read works. In it, he told this parable:

> There are these two young fish swimming along and they happen to meet an older fish swimming the other way, who nods at them and says, "Morning, boys. How's the water?" The two young fish say nothing, swim on for a bit, and then eventually one turns to the other and says, "What the hell is water?"[1]

Over the last decade, as I've worked with businesses across the world on their content marketing strategy, the most common first question

I've heard is this: "What do you mean by content?" In business, content is water.

Welcome to content marketing strategy

Before we begin to implement, it seems important to define the three words that make up this book's title. You've no doubt thumbed (or scrolled) through this book, eyed the chapter headings, and asked yourself, "What exactly is content marketing strategy?"

Well, let's back up even further and first ask, "What exactly is a business?" Since content marketing strategy applies to an approach that helps our business, it seems sensible to know what we're solving for.

The good news is we have great shoulders to stand on for this definition. The wonderful author and renowned business strategist Peter Drucker defined a business as "a social group that differs from other social groups in only one way: businesses must have customers."[2]

Of course, there are other bits that comprise a business: products and services, a marketplace to showcase them, and the processes, activities, and norms by which the social group operates. Finally, a business includes one other inextricable thing (and I would argue it's the most important): content.

Content is key... and it's (almost) everywhere

Content is every business's core operating system. It is the connective tissue that ties all the bits together. If a business is a social group, content is the communication that enables it to be social.

Content is the body of knowledge that describes the activities and norms by which the business operates. It's the main ingredient of the experiences created to showcase products in the marketplace, and it is core to helping customers derive the most value from the product or service that is sold.

Content is communication. It's all around us all the time.

Strategy puts purpose behind communication

Now let's look at each word of this book's title. We start with the last word because it's the most important.

I see too many managers struggle to rationalize putting a *strategy* around content. Managing the entirety of a business's content can seem unachievable; it's like the fish trying to figure out how to manage water. Unsurprisingly, many executives don't consider it the best use of time or money.

They rationalize their hesitation by saying that trying to define all the content doesn't make sense. It's too overwhelming. However, that doesn't mean that managers don't try to control some *parts* of the content. In fact, whenever most businesses try to apply an initial "strategy" to their marketing, the typical first step is to place much tighter controls on who is allowed to create content, what they will create, and how they will do it, for very specific parts of the business (usually marketing, PR, and sales to start).

What happens? Well, businesses' brand managers begin to write messaging guidelines, SEO keyword standards, sales scripts, and standardized value propositions to try to define and set the words and phrases that should and shouldn't be used in marketing and sales communications.

Now, it's not that documenting these ideas is unproductive. The mistake is conflating the documentation itself with the strategy. Businesses look at trying to define how to swim in some small part of the water as the strategy, instead of coordinating the strength to swim in all water. As I said before, the content itself provides no strategic value.

"Now, wait a minute!" a CMO once said, interrupting me. "What is a content *strategy*, and how does it provide any competitive advantage if the content itself does not? Isn't the strategy supposed to define the content?"

We can climb up on the shoulders of Harvard Business School professor Michael Porter for a perfectly capable definition of the word "strategy." A strategy, according to Porter, is the creation of a "fit" among all the things that are done in the company—establishing a unique and valuable position, involving *different* sets of activities that require establishing priorities (or trade-offs):

- Serve the *few* needs of *many* customers.
- Serve the *broad* needs of *few* customers.
- Serve the *broad* needs of *many* customers in a *narrow* market.[3]

A competitive strategy requires a business to make these trade-offs in where they compete, and to make decisions about what they WON'T do as a social group after making these trade-offs. A strategy's chances of *success* depend on creating that broader "fit" (or alignment) among all the activities the company decides to perform after making these decisions.

Put simply: A successful strategy fits together the activities in a business that help everyone in the business work toward a common goal. As you might already have guessed, "activities" are the important part of that breakdown. As Porter says, "Ultimately, all differences between companies... derive from the hundreds of activities required [to run the business]... **Activities then are the basic units of competitive advantage.**"[4]

However, Porter also observes a difference between activities that drive simple operational effectiveness (OE), which he defines as "performing similar activities better than rivals," and strategy, which is performing *different* activities than rivals or performing similar activities in different ways.

Essentially, competitive strategy is not just figuring out how to do the same activities more efficiently. It is fitting together *different* activities, or the same activities performed in *different* ways, that creates a differentiating strategy.

OK. Now that we've defined strategy, we can begin to see the connection between a business's content and the concept of having a strategy for it.

So, bringing it back to the conversation I had with that CMO colleague, I answered:

> A great content strategy is not trying to describe the water around us in a way that states, "This is how the brand will talk about topics X, Y, or Z." Rather, a great content strategy is the coordination of all

the *different activities* required to enable a business to communicate effectively. Full stop. A company's perfect content strategy coordinates the different activities in a way that enables the entire organization to clearly communicate whatever it wants to communicate, whenever it wants to communicate it.

That gets us to the word in the book title that bridges the ideas of content and strategy.

Marketing qualifies and focuses our efforts

Once we conclude that content is communication and strategy is the coordination of different activities to create competitive advantage, the last task is to define *which activities* we are talking about.

Well, for the purposes of this book: marketing.

Tackling all content-related activities and how the business communicates holistically is a lot to take on at once for most businesses—and is beyond the scope of this book. Thus, we need to focus our efforts. The activities associated with external marketing and communications are a prime and optimal place to start. Why? As established in the previous section, that's where businesses are prone to start their efforts to control content creation.

But now we must define marketing as well.

For that, we can lean on one of my marketing heroes, Philip Kotler— author, consultant, and the distinguished professor of international marketing at the Kellogg School of Management at Northwestern University. He was also kind enough to write the foreword to this book, and I'll tell you that this was a "bucket list" item for me.

Kotler describes marketing as "the science and art of exploring, creating, and delivering value to satisfy the needs of a target market at a profit."[5]

I love that definition.

Kotler explains that each of the words in that definition has a specific meaning and, in his explanations, you begin to hear a connection, a tether, between content and strategy that starts to define a very specific purpose: a content marketing purpose, if you will. He discusses how marketing is a co-creation of content with consumers, getting deep into the challenges we face as communicators today. He discusses how marketers today must move beyond "mind share" and "heart share" to develop a "spirit share"—a share "of something a little more than narrow to your own interests" where we are "creating emotional relationships that's [sic] more than limited to the person's own nurturing of his or her ego."[6]

In other words, Kotler is encouraging us as marketers to fit activities together that do more than feed the consumer's ego, or claim that our organization is socially responsible, or propose that our products are the best alternative in the marketplace. He is encouraging marketers to create content that has tangible value beyond just the attributes of the service or product we offer. He's encouraging what we would call content marketing as a core approach to marketing.

That leads us to a definition of what we're discussing:

> **Content marketing strategy**—a marketing discipline that is the sum of all the activities required to enable a business to consistently communicate in a way that creates tangible value for target audiences. It is what enables a brand to have not only a voice but also something to say that is worth listening to.

Content marketing strategy is not just a different kind of content. It is a different set of activities—a well-coordinated operation—that enables the business to create any kind of content that delivers value to both audiences and the business it serves.

So, again: The content you create for your business provides no sustainable competitive advantage. But a coordinated content marketing strategy just might.

Content marketing strategy: An approach for the next decade

In the mid-1990s, something happened that changed marketing strategy (and the entirety of promotional strategies) forever. You might think I mean the internet or, more specifically, the World Wide Web. But that's not exactly it.

The internet and the web certainly became the fastest-growing new medium for accessing media. But it was the introduction of one specific function that changed the entire foundation of media on the web and birthed the fundamental change in both marketing and buyer behavior.

In a word: search.

Until this point, marketers depended almost exclusively on a one-way street of media to reach audiences. Broadcast or cable TV, radio, print, or websites were the only channels to reach large, aggregate audiences. Successful marketers identified which of these limited options had the highest likely concentration of their desired audience. Then they aligned their advertising or promotional content to appear on these channels and made bets on the type of content that would have the highest chance of influencing them.

Search changed all that. This new tool made one-to-one reach and frequency not only possible but also a much better way of interacting with audiences. With search, marketing managers didn't have to guess which audiences were watching which programs or at what time they watched them. They didn't have to worry about how many times they needed to air a message on a channel. They could be "on" 24/7/365. Brands could now optimize their own media—their websites—to be more easily *found* whenever buyers searched for their product or service.

Marketers, in theory, could circumvent the waste of paying for placing their message on broadcast media altogether. The race was on for who could build the most robust, informational content experiences optimized for being found against any query and then build one-to-one relationships with those visitors.

But it didn't quite work out that way. You see, when everybody gets that same memo, it turns out it's not so simple. From a marketer's viewpoint, search made a one-to-one relationship with *buyers* possible. In the earliest days of search, it only captured people who already knew their need or want. So, by definition, competing businesses were all vying for that sliver of time when any one customer was in a "buying mood" and searching for a product or service. The game became to compete to be the first search result returned for a given query. Google found they could monetize that game through allowing people to purchase that top spot for the highest bid and built a trillion-dollar business on the back of this extraordinarily simple idea.

Thus, even for modern marketing strategies, getting to the top of search was expensive, and so it still made sense to buy advertising on TV, print, radio, and the internet, because marketers needed to also convince customers to get into a "buying mood" and make that search.

By 2010, marketing strategists also discovered that search, the advancing evolution of social media, and the increasing availability of both mobile and wired bandwidth created another new behavior in consumers. People search not just for things to purchase, but for everything: on-demand education, entertainment, inspiration, and value. The web, and the burgeoning quantity of content on it, became not just a utility for commerce but also disruptive competition for traditional entertainment, education, and all other forms of media consumption. And search and social media enabled an entirely new way to navigate all that media.

That was when businesses discovered that through search and social, they could go beyond *leveraging* the popular media that people were interested in finding and actually *become* the media that people were interested in finding.

Energy drink brand Red Bull may be one of the best-known examples of a company that embraced this new model of engaging customers. Through a variety of content efforts started in the early 2000s, by 2010 Red Bull had secured one of the most loyal audiences in digital media.

As Brian Morrissey from the marketing publication *Digiday* said in an article from 2012:

> The Austrian energy drink brand cemented itself as the Coke of the
> shareable content era, willing to spend freely to produce content so
> good that it is indistinguishable from non-marketing content. Red Bull
> truly is a media company that happens to sell soft drinks.[7]

Brands of all kinds discovered an alternative to renting space on traditional media companies' "real estate." They discovered that they, too, could compete more effectively in search and social media for the attention, subscription, and loyalty of audiences so that even be-fore people realize they have a need or want, the brand's offerings are the first (and perhaps only) solution they consider.

Enter the concept of modern content marketing.

In 2011, I co-wrote one of the first books on content marketing, *Managing Content Marketing*. In the foreword, Jeffrey Hayzlett, the former CMO of Kodak and bestselling author, called it "the road map and fail-safe process for content marketing."[8]

We could never have anticipated just how important and inte-grated this new approach would become in modern business. Content marketing has become a critical enhancement to every other market-ing and communications practice: from internal employee communi-cations to public relations and corporate communications, analyst relations, customer service and loyalty, and, of course, direct market-ing and sales efforts.

Over the ensuing decade, my team and I have studied and worked with hundreds of brands all over the world on their content marketing efforts. Every year since 2011, the Content Marketing Institute has issued comprehensive research on the practice of content marketing.

As we enter hip-deep into the second decade of modern content marketing, it's time to look again at how it has become part of a broader disruption in marketing and sales. In 2011, Joe and I pre-dicted that at some point content marketing would not be considered a separate approach, but rather a core discipline within the broader practice of a marketing strategy.

That has become true. However, we should not forget Porter's def-inition of strategy as the creation of a fit between all activities. There are indeed *different activities* involved in content marketing. And when businesses fail at content marketing it is because they try to apply the same, classic activities from direct marketing and sales to the approach of content marketing.

In 2023 and beyond, three fundamental trends will create the op-portunity for a more optimal set of activities around content, market-ing, and strategy.

What are those trends?

Trend #1: The supply-induced scarcity of physical presence

The first trend is something my team and I have been calling the supply-induced scarcity of physical presence. Now that is, indeed, what my dad used to call a bunch of 10-dollar words. But I haven't found anything better to describe what is going on.

To put it more simply, in business, consumers have seen their threshold of willingness to participate in physical experiences become higher and more precious. The global pandemic certainly accelerated and exacerbated this trend, and factors such as remote work, the decline of business travel, and the gig economy will all certainly continue to play an important role in its durability.

For example, businesses that operate in sectors that require the most intense levels of physical presence (healthcare, retail, banks, delivery services, leisure, and travel) are undergoing fundamental digital transformation. Disruptions such as e-commerce and more interactive digital experiences are changing the requirements (and necessity) for physical presence.

What all that means is that we (as consumers) value our physical presence a lot more than we used to. That's why this is a supply-induced scarcity. The demand for our time and physical presence may continue to be high—but our desire to give it will be much lower.

The implications of this larger trend are twofold. The first is that the physical experiences businesses design will have to become much more remarkable. The bar will be higher for a business's next retail experience, customer conference, team meeting, or in-person sales presentation.

The second implication—much more relevant to marketers—is that digital, content-driven experiences now must act as a proxy for many of the physical experiences we used to take for granted. So, there is even more pressure on marketing and communications teams to produce more digital content experiences at every part of the customer's journey.

Marketing teams will be asked to create exponentially more content in the coming years. The pressure to operate like a media company will only intensify. Yes, that means that the activities businesses begin to fit together to respond to this trend will become an increasingly meaning-ful part of whether they will succeed in any marketing and communi-cations strategy.

Content marketing is becoming a core piece of the entirety of busi-ness communications. That leads to the second disruption.

Trend #2: The return of "push" content

In the earliest days of the internet, content was simply discovered through whatever platform the user happened to use. You got what you got. For example, if you signed on through America Online (AOL) you would see whatever AOL had available. That content was technically delivered over the internet, but it was pushed to you based on whatever the platform thought was most important. It sounds almost ridiculous now, but if you made it out of your walled garden of AOL to the wildly unorganized World Wide Web, you could use a new kind of program called a "browser" to "surf the web." You would just browse web pages, and hopefully something interesting would attract your attention.

Similarly, the internet's first popular search engine, Yahoo, was simply a directory of websites that Yahoo had indexed. You were not truly searching the internet but rather the limited content that Yahoo had gotten around to trying to organize.

As I mentioned before, all that changed quickly once Google en-tered the picture.

Over the last two decades, we've seen an unfathomable amount of content added to the internet. By some estimates we now add 2.5 quin-tillion bytes of data to the internet every single day. That number is so large that it defies our ability to comprehend it. Searchable content has become the defining interface to just about everything. In the modern world, there is no purpose for television program guides or printed phone directories. Products today often don't even ship with printed user manuals that are out of date, expensive to produce, and easily lost. It's just easier to search for what you need help with, and find the latest and most updated instructions.

However, in 2023, almost exactly 25 years since Google brought its search platform online, we have reached another milestone in the way we consume content. There is now so much content available, and so much competition for those top spots, that even search has become inefficient.

Content discovery is changing the way we interact with digital content. New research, as detailed in *Search Engine Journal* (SEJ), shows that 30 percent of search users are now "forced to redo their search queries in order to find what they're looking for."[9] Audiences have become increasingly frustrated with the results from Google and other search engines. But why?

It's because businesses have spent the last decade producing more and more content designed to rank higher against search queries. This led Google to attempt to put more and more information (the actual answers) on the search results page itself. This means that the most "popular answer" is often the one given at the top of a search result, and this leads to bad answers to smart questions. Thus, as some users have exclaimed, it seems that "Google gets dumber by the day."

Interestingly, this conclusion is wrong. Google is not getting dumber; Google is actually becoming smarter. The "wrong" results are an early indicator of Google attempting to provide better answers than the vast quantity of "SEO-optimized" content is providing. Google is trying to understand not what you asked for, but what you really want.

Here's an example: You ask Google for the number of calories in a loaf of bread and it returns the nutritional information for a *slice* of bread. That isn't because Google doesn't know the number of calories in a loaf of bread; it's because Google knows (from its exceedingly large set of behavioral data) that you're much more likely to want to know the total calories in a slice, not a loaf.

This is content discovery version 2.0—much smarter than when the web first started.

Content discovery will be an increasingly important aspect of how audiences consume content. TikTok is the first platform wholly designed around this evolution in a meaningful way. Algorithms and artificial intelligence platforms are now so powerful that, combined with the data generated from the huge amount of time we spend online, content we want is being pushed to us before we even know we want it.

This is beginning to happen in entertainment: Netflix recommends programs to us based on our viewing habits, and Amazon suggests books (and other products) based on our purchase and browsing history.

Further, newer artificial intelligence (AI)-focused technologies are now automatically creating content for us. Technologies such as ChatGPT, Dall-E2, and Stable Diffusion are now not only providing platforms to generate original content based on queries, they are incorporated into search, to push confident answers to queries instead of options of destinations. And guess what? Right now those answers are just as "bad" and incorrect as the search engines are.

Businesses will begin to deal with this as well. As the customer journey evolves into more targeted, personalized experiences at all stages, marketers will need to evolve into creating advanced content displays to help anticipate customers' needs and deliver the value they want before they even know they want it.

You might think it means we have to develop *yet more content.*

It's true. But, here's the thing. In this case, creating more won't be enough.

For the last several years, businesses have been trying to react to this pressure for "more content" by building in-house content studios or content marketing teams. In many cases, businesses even call these teams "content factories." The Association of National Advertisers released research in 2018 that noted that "the explosive growth of in-house agencies is one of the most significant trends in the advertising and marketing industry today." They noted that 78 percent of companies have an in-house agency, and that content marketing is offered by 75 percent of those in-house agencies.[10]

Brands feel as though they can scale to the need of "more" simply by building a function to support the production of more words, pictures, video, audio, etc. But it's not working. Why?

This gets me to something I call Robert's Content Law: The need for more content assets increases in direct proportion to the increase in the number of resources solely allocated to creating more assets.

In other words, trying to build the capability to always deliver "more" content immediately sets us off on the wrong foot. Businesses cannot ever scale to a total of "more" because "more" will always be needed. Rather, brands must begin to operate like a strategic media company and build an activity around the question of "How much is enough?"

That's a *different* activity—and one that can create a competitive advantage, because it implicitly asks the question that starts to force us to plan and prioritize: "Enough *of what*?"

Push content and the evolution of artificial intelligence and the media bring us to the third modern disruption.

Trend #3: The decline of trust and truth

In many ways, it feels as if the world today is more divided than ever. And honestly, in 2023, it's hard to know in the moment whether it's getting better or worse. We do know that trust in institutions is as low as it's ever been. Whether it's government, mainstream media, businesses, or even nonprofits, we are awash with misinformation and mistrust of our institutions, our leaders, and even our peers.

Further, it's not just new misinformation that causes a challenge for trust and truth. Because new artificial intelligence engines use existing repositories of content (such as the internet) for their learning models, we are being reminded just how inaccurate and untrustworthy the internet can be. Every time an AI engine confidently returns an inaccurate fact, or complete misinformation, it's because it learned it from an unreliable learning source.

While there is much to discuss that is bigger than business and content marketing, we should recognize that these disruptions are part of a bigger trend that can help us shape the future of content and marketing.

When the bar of trust is so low, marketers have not just an opportunity but a *responsibility* to take societal leadership and develop trust and truth as a core skill.

As Kotler told us, great marketing adds value that customers invest in and that can create wealth for the business. But not all that customer investment must involve a purchase of our traditional products or services.

Every year for the last decade, the PR firm Edelman has published its Trust Barometer research. It examines the state of trust globally and assigns a score on what consumers trust when it comes to institutions. The headline for 2023: "Social fabric weakens amid deepening divisions." And their conclusion is that "a lack of faith in societal institutions triggered by economic anxiety, disinformation, mass-class divide and a failure of leadership has brought us where we are today—deeply and dangerously polarized."[11]

But again, very much like physical presence, this doesn't mean the *demand* for trust and truth is low—it just means the *supply* is scarce. Consumers don't just look more favorably on businesses that take a leadership position on societal issues; they now expect the company to communicate that position well.

These days, more than ever before, we will choose a product, a service, an employer, or an investment based on the company's values and ability to communicate them. If there has ever been a more important time for businesses to coordinate their communication and ensure that they tell a powerful, valuable, and trustworthy story, I can't think of it. In 2023 and beyond, content marketing is no longer just an interesting alternative to advertising and direct marketing. It is now a *responsibility* of any successful business. Coordinated content marketing is as important as—or even arguably more important than—the products or services put into the marketplace.

A company with any kind of competitive advantage will also have a well-defined set of different activities (processes) associated with making, distributing, and managing its products and services. This isn't hard to imagine.

Content is just as important. What does this mean?

It means a business-wide approach to leaning into trust, privacy, and the use of our customers' data (commonly called first-party data). It means a set of different activities for gathering customer information and personalizing experiences to deliver deeper value. Instead of looking at personal data as a means of "selling more," businesses should look to data acquisition as a mechanism to deliver enhanced value (content discovery).

If a business is still worrying about how to gate content (requiring an email address to access marketing content) in a siloed system for lead generation, but has a different system for holding their customer data, and yet a third for signing up to get access to a training or library of how to get the most out of its products and services—that business is well behind in the trust game.

It's not good enough anymore to put a "cookie notice" on the website and think audiences will trust us more. They are well aware that "accepting cookies" is not a real choice. It merely calls attention to the fact that a company is assembling data so it can sell to them. The strategy behind audience data is not an IT or a legal challenge. It is a content challenge. It's now our turn as marketers.

We have to be okay with a wider charter. We must be willing to become experts on the use of first-party audience data and ensure the privacy and trust of our customers. It's a *new* activity for us.

The end of better content as the new business case

Too often, content marketers get wrapped up in what content they are creating rather than their ability to lead the efforts to create it.

One of my go-to books of the last decade is Rita Gunther McGrath's *The End of Competitive Advantage.* She is a teacher with a huge influence on my work. In that book, she vividly illustrates that all competitive advantage is transient, and perhaps now more than ever. This fact, she contends, is understood. But then she asks, "Why hasn't basic strategy practice changed?" As she says:

> Most executives, even when they realize that competitive advantages are going to be ephemeral, are still using strategy frameworks and tools designed for achieving a sustainable competitive advantage, not for quickly exploiting and moving in and out of advantages.[12]

The last part of that has the deepest implications for the evolving practice of strategic content marketing in a business. After having the privilege of working with hundreds of enterprise brands over the last 10 years, I've concluded: **Most businesses think about how they can change content to fit marketing's purpose instead of how they might change marketing to fit content's purpose.**

As I said at the beginning of this chapter, content itself will never be a sustainable competitive advantage or differentiator—all content is easily replicable, and its differentiated value is, at best, only transient.

Instead, consider a business case for a content marketing *operation* as the catalyst that can change everything for the content marketing challenges you face. Recognize that you and the activities you perform *are* the competitive advantage. Critical to future success is your ability as a team (of one or 100) to be dynamic and fluid—moving in and out of "arenas" (as McGrath calls them) of content and creating temporary advantages.

Here's the real takeaway. If you agree with this business case for a content marketing strategy, and as you start into the following chapters, ask everyone in your business—including your CEO—if they truly believe that compelling, engaging, useful, and dynamic content-driven experiences will move the business forward.

If the answer is yes, then realize your *strategic* value is in your ability to evolve and coordinate all the activities to repeatedly create those valuable experiences. It is not the content itself or where you distribute it. Put simply: The content marketing team's job is not to be good at content; it is to enable the business to be good at content.

I now recognize that one of the first signs of trouble in any strategic content marketing approach is if the first question is, "*How do we get more efficient at content?*"

Getting to efficiency assumes there is a working, standard operation that is providing value. The goal is then to change that process to remove the friction. But when there's no repeatable, standard operation, focusing on efficiency is simply trying to produce the same or more content with the same or fewer resources.

Neither usually works out to be better for the business.

The more difficult task is to determine the *different* activities the business will do to create, or augment, the processes in place, or which activities the business will do differently.

Your business's content capabilities reflect its ability to communicate. And your ability to evolve the activities impacting communication is, indeed, the only thing that creates any competitive advantage.

The content you create will provide no sustainable competitive advantage. But a strategic content marketing strategy just might.

At the end of the graduation speech I mentioned at the beginning of this chapter, David Foster Wallace came back to the fish-in-water story. He summed up his primary lesson from it by saying:

> It's about the real value of real education, which has almost nothing to do with knowledge and everything to do with simple awareness; awareness of what is so real and essential, so hidden in plain sight all around us, all the time, that we have to keep reminding ourselves over and over: This is water. This is water.[13]

The real value of a content marketing strategy has almost nothing to do with the content we create day to day and everything to do with the awareness of how content is essential to the entire business, how it connects everything all around us that makes up the business. It's not about better defining one part of the water we swim in; it's helping us all be better swimmers in water. To do that, we have to keep reminding ourselves over and over: "This is content. This is content."

If you're ready, it's now time to jump in the water and build our modern content marketing strategy.

Notes

1 Wallace, D.F. (2009) *This Is Water*, New York: Little, Brown, p.1

2 Drucker, P.F. (1973) *Management: Tasks, responsibilities, practices*, New York: Harper & Row, p.58

3 Porter, M.E. (1996) What Is Strategy? *Harvard Business Review*, https://hbr.org/1996/11/what-is-strategy (archived at https://perma.cc/2ZZZ-R7BG)

4 Ibid, emphasis added

5 Kotler, P. (2019) Kotler Marketing Group, Inc, https://kotlermarketing.com/phil_questions.shtml (archived at https://perma.cc/FS88-6MPH)

6 Luck, I. (2019) Philip Kotler: Marketing Strategy, www.marketingstrategy.com/videos/philip-kotler-marketing-strategy/ (archived at https://perma.cc/KQ9S-JXSM)

7 Morrissey, B. (2012) What Red Bull can teach content marketers, *Digiday*, https://digiday.com/marketing/what-red-bull-can-teach-content-marketers/ (archived at https://perma.cc/U8LQ-KVER)

8 Pulizzi, J., Rose, R., and Hayzlett, J. (2011) *Managing Content Marketing: The real-world guide for creating passionate subscribers to your brand*, Cleveland, OH: McGraw-Hill Education, p.6.

9 Montti, R. (2022) Research finds evidence of user dissatisfaction with Google results, *Search Engine Journal*, www.searchenginejournal.com/research-finds-evidence-of-user-dissatisfaction-with-google-results/469539/ (archived at https://perma.cc/9LYX-PKTH)

10 ANA (2018) The continued rise of the in-house agency, www.ana.net/miccontent/show/id/rr-2018-in-house-agency (archived at https://perma.cc/63SS-Z63F)

11 Edelman (2023) 2023 Edelman Trust Barometer, www.edelman.com/trust/2023/trust-barometer (archived at https://perma.cc/D2U6-89KE)

12 Gunther McGrath, R. (2013) *The End of Competitive Advantage: How to keep your strategy moving as fast as your business*, Boston, MA: Harvard Business Review Press, p.7

13 Wallace, D.F. (2009) *This Is Water*, New York: Little, Brown, p.144

The Three Pillars 02
Understanding the Fundamental Elements of a Successful Content Marketing Strategy

In most businesses content is everybody's job, and no one's strategy.

All happy marketers are alike. But every unhappy marketer is unhappy in their own way.

I stole that line from Tolstoy; it's modeled after the first line of *Anna Karenina*. But it's perfect for the state of today's marketing strategy and a great place to begin our strategy-building journey. The idea—now often called the Anna Karenina principle—is that happy groups of people are happy because of a common set of attributes. But any variety of attributes can cause an unhappy group.

In my three decades of experience with the tension between marketing teams and the rest of the business, I have found the Anna Karenina principle to be true. When marketers are working successfully with other teams in the business, they have a similar way of working. But when marketing fails, it is almost always a unique series of challenges that keeps them unhappy.

To understand where content marketing is today and what makes a happy content marketing team (even if it's a team of one), we need to first understand how marketing became a functional (sometimes dysfunctional) operation within businesses, and then how modern content marketing can provide a common way of integrating into it.

The origins of what has been called the "marketing mix" go back to 1948 when a Harvard University marketing professor, James Culliton, published an article describing marketers as "mixers of ingredients."[1]

He compared marketers to bartenders who would mix the requisite efforts that might go into a great-tasting "cocktail" of a marketing strategy.

This concept went the 1950s version of viral and became an incredibly popular framework for constructing a marketing strategy. However, there was a problem. While marketers could agree that they were the "mixers of ingredients," no one could agree on what the right ingredients were.

In 1960, Jerome McCarthy—another marketing professor—wrote a book called *Basic Marketing: A managerial approach* to try to set a standard for those ingredients. In it, he introduced a framework you may be familiar with but don't use much any longer—the 4 Ps.

This concept became, arguably, even more famous than the "marketing mix." The 4 Ps—product, place, price, and promotion—became a core focus of marketing education and practice for decades.

Figure 2.1   The 4 Ps

PRODUCT
The description of the product or service. The features, quality, branding, and packaging. The "ingredients."

PLACE
The distribution strategy for the product. Where it will be available for purchase.

PRICE
Pricing strategy, allowances, discounts, payment terms, or bulk purchase rates.

PROMOTION
Balancing where to promote and how frequently promotion is repeated.

NOTE The 4 Ps—also known as the marketing mix—was a foundational model used to describe how marketers were "mixers of ingredients" (or activities) that would form the basis of a smart marketing strategy.

- **Product** was the effort you put into the offering itself. This included the features, benefits, packaging, variety of colors—all the things that you would normally associate with optimizing what is being sold.

- **Place** was "where" you would offer the product or service. This included all the distribution strategies, including wholesale, retail, e-commerce, regional markets, etc.

- **Price** included the pricing strategies and where and how discounts might be included, or the different methods of pricing based on volume discounts. Then, finally . . .

- **Promotion** was the strategy and plan for getting the word out in the right media channels. The promotion ingredients included the plans for advertising vs. PR vs. sales enablement along with the messaging strategy and frequency to reach the right number of potential customers.[2]

For most businesses today, "promotion" is the bulk of the marketing mix. Pricing, place, and product are usually left to other disciplines within the business such as product management, product marketing, sales, research, or even senior leadership.

But that doesn't mean the marketer's job has become smaller. Quite the contrary. While the scope of the 4 Ps has been reduced to only promotion, most marketing teams now have to account for promotional activities across the entirety of the customer's journey: from unaware and unreached through to sales, successful onboarding, and even loyalty, upsell, cross-sell, and referral. Modern marketing, as a practice, has evolved from a largely inward-focused function working to optimize a product or service for sale in a marketplace to an outward-focused communications function meant to enhance the value of the entire organization at every step of the customer's journey. As you can probably guess, that means marketing's responsibility for different forms of communication (content) has expanded exponentially.

Marketing's focus: Reach and frequency

Within the promotion part of McCarthy's framework, the core of that ingredient is the concept of where to put the message and how many times to repeat it. In other words: What content will we create, and how many times do people need to consume it before they are persuaded to change the behavior we want changed?

This idea became known as "reach and frequency." "Reach" identifies and plans which media channels a marketer should use to promote a message to the largest audience with the most potential to be impacted. "Frequency" is balancing the number of times a marketer needs to repeat that message until it creates the desired impact.

Thus, our overarching goal as marketers has become clear: Balance reach and frequency to optimize costs against the impact (or value) we can create with content.

While we want to reach as many in our target market as possible, our goal is to do it as infrequently as possible while still achieving the desired impact. Why? Because while reach is *value* to our business, frequency represents *cost*. As a marketer, if I have to pay to run my content on television, radio, or print multiple times, it costs more. If I make more cold calls, it costs more. If I have to buy more billboard space across a city, it costs more. Put simply: The more times I have to say something, the more it costs.

So, why does understanding marketing history help our approach to today's content marketing strategy?

Because today, most businesses still measure their marketing strategy based on this history and the three letters it has come to represent: ROI (return on investment). For most businesses the entire calculation for the marketing budget is about efficiency. How many people can we impact, as infrequently as possible, in order to meet our business objectives?

Is it any wonder that many businesses look at the marketing expense line the same way they look at the tax line? One CEO said to me once, "I wish I could cheat my marketing costs as easily as I cheat my taxes."

Over the decades, the art and science of reach and frequency have become a foundational piece of how marketers strategize their campaigns across the range of marketing disciplines. It was the pillar of the practice of media planning and the fuel for the astronomical growth of agencies and consulting firms from the 1950s through today. The role of the "ad agency" became one of helping marketers handle the marketing mix of promotion—optimizing spend by getting the most out of reach and frequency to create sales results.

In fact, the term "working media" became a standard rule in marketing and advertising. Working media is the percentage of an advertiser's budget spent on distributing their content to an audience (the frequency): In other words, the budget for placing your message on all those other platforms. Non-working media was what you spent on things like creating content, agency fees, and design costs. The general rule was that non-working media should never be more than about 15–20 percent of total advertising spend.

But a funny thing happened as content marketing came to the forefront of marketing and advertising strategies. Marketing managers learned that "owned media" could be working media as well. If they could somehow *become* the working media that was traditionally paid for, and they could attract and engage the same audience, then the entire rule and framework of reach and frequency and "working media" shift in their favor. This idea requires a new framework.

An old discipline remade for the 21st century

One story you'll hear more about in the pages that follow is that of Victor Gao. The company he worked for until July 2022, Arrow Electronics, is in the top 150 of the Fortune 500, has more than $24 billion in annual revenue, and has been an industry leader for more than 80 years.

From 2012 to 2014, Arrow Electronics watched as the specialized publications it heavily advertised in began to go out of business one by one. These publications were how Arrow's customers, electrical engineers, kept up with developments in the industry—and how kids became enamored with the field and were inspired to become electrical engineers. These publications are, quite literally, the lifeline for increasing the knowledge and total addressable market of the Arrow Electronics customer base.

And so the concern for the publications and their health was real. As Victor said in an interview with us for our book *Killing Marketing*, "Many of these niche publications are buried in the belly of much larger media conglomerates."[3] Publishing about electronics may not be their highest priority.

Arrow seized this opportunity. It saw the tremendous need to serve engineers. Where the big media conglomerates couldn't afford to digitize small-circulation print magazines, Arrow could. Where the success of niche-oriented publications wasn't in the interest of the media parent companies, it was directly linked to Arrow's success.

By the end of 2016, Arrow Electronics had established itself as the largest media company in electronics. In February 2015, Arrow purchased 16 engineering websites, e-newsletters, inventory access tools, and databases from Hearst's United Technical Publishing.[4] One year later, the company acquired the entire electronics media portfolio of UBM, including the brands EE Times, EDN, SEM, Embedded, EBN, TechOnline, and DataSheets.com for $23.5 million.[5]

The content and marketing portfolio for Arrow Electronics sells advertising to competitors and partners, holds events, and develops educational content for electronics professionals. The effort is 100 percent on developing value for the consumer. As Gao told us in that same interview, "I can tell you that we're highly profitable. But we reinvest that money into the editorial coverage and into the product experience."

That is a great content marketing strategy.

One can see how content marketing provides more value to consumers across a more expansive view of the customer's journey—and through an "owned media" strategy. From driving awareness of a new idea to deepening trust in a brand, driving sales, and creating a more loyal customer, content marketing has always been a part of helping to drive extended value and trust in marketing.

Content marketing as a function is a new and core part of McCarthy's 4 Ps—squarely in the promotion ingredient of the modern marketing mix. Media strategy has gone beyond paid media (advertising), shared media (social media), and earned media (public relations). Owned media has entered the marketing strategy lexicon.

"Working media" now includes a business's own media channels such as resource centers, educational platforms, communities, blogs, digital magazines, email newsletters, podcasts, video series, and even digital and physical events.

But the critical factor is that a successful content marketing strategy consists of different activities and a different model than reach and frequency. How do businesses create, manage, scale, and measure all their activities in order to be able to operate like a media company at a profit? It requires that all of the various marketing teams, from brand teams to digital marketing, demand generation, field marketing, advertising agencies, and even customer service, all work together. There is only one problem.

Marketing is more siloed now than ever before

Twenty-five years after the digital and search revolution, marketing teams have kicked content production into high gear. Websites, blogs, landing pages, email, social media, mobile technologies, and so many other content-driven experiences power the approaches for businesses everywhere. But, no surprise, there has been a struggle over how to manage the overwhelming amounts of new digital media that this approach requires.

Technology vendors have tried to come to the rescue. Marketing automation sprang up as a concept to offer a better way to manage and automate email channels. Web content management systems emerged to manage big, complex websites. As websites became more dated, and things like microsites, resource centers, blogs, and e-commerce came along, these solutions subsequently re-branded themselves as "digital experience" platforms. Then, digital asset management emerged to manage the huge repositories of rich media digital files created by marketing teams. Social media suites enabled the management of content on third-party social platforms.

But because these content tools were focused primarily by channel, digital teams began to be similarly siloed. The teams that worked with these tools became "email teams" or "web teams" or "social teams." Today, it's not uncommon to see entire marketing teams siloed by the tools or channels that they are responsible for.

This siloed nature of digital encouraged content marketing to become a tactical function within these teams, consisting of one-off projects that sometimes worked and sometimes didn't. Content marketing became every marketer's job, but no one's strategy. There was no framework or common set of standards for how the business communicated value except at discrete steps along the customer's journey. The brand team manages the website but doesn't communicate with the demand generation team that manages the blog and the resource center. The demand generation team doesn't collaborate with the customer service team that manages the customer community and the help microsite. The social team is off in its own world managing its channels. And the PR team is relegated to continuing to try to develop news about the company that will get covered elsewhere.

It's a mess.

Successful brands are balancing their marketing and content strategies. They realize they must move beyond the reach and frequency model to cover and scale valuable content that connects every step across the entire customer journey. They have realized that specific, new frameworks and operational functions exist that would enable them to operate more like media companies and get their arms around the complexities of unifying the entirety of marketing and communications content.

In other words, the activities—the content operations—make up a core piece of how great marketing departments evolve and scale their ability to create differentiated content-driven experiences.

To create these new activities and transform them into repeatable processes, we can, and must, see content marketing in a new strategic framework.

The three pillars of content marketing strategy

Just as we have the 4 Ps to describe the overall marketing mix, we require a new model to describe the strategy of content marketing.

The content marketing strategy begins with three core pillars: Communication, Experiences, and Operations (which bridges the other two). These pillars overlap slightly and thus frame five specific categories of activities that managers in the business will perform.

Following are descriptions of the pillars and their associated activities.

1: *Coordinated communication*

As we established at the beginning of this book, business content is communication. So, the business must perform certain activities to better coordinate the use of content in order to acquire, keep, and grow customers and other audiences.

A successful business communicates clearly and with a consistent voice. It is also able to communicate in creative and uniquely relevant ways that reflect the diversity of its people and audiences. To achieve that delicate balance of consistency and diversity, coordination is critical. This means that the first core category of activities in the communication pillar is Purpose. This is content-as-a-capability. Many businesses fall into a trap because they believe that content

Figure 2.2   The Three Pillars of Content Marketing Strategy

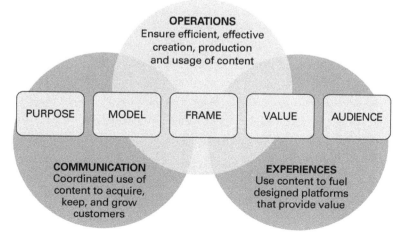

NOTE These three pillars, and subsequently the business's ability to successfully apply the five categories of activities within them, make up the pressure points of a strong content marketing strategy.

marketing can simply be created as a "skill position" within the business. They hire a few journalists, editors, creative copywriters, and subject matter experts, and set them off to be "good" at creating and managing valuable content.

But, as I said in the previous chapter, businesses that are managing successful content marketing strategies realize that the primary purpose of a capable content team is not to be good at creating content. It is, rather, to enable the *business* to be good at the operation of content. Those journalists, creative copywriters, or subject matter experts are usually thrown into a business with only the task to "create great stuff." There is usually no shortage of that demand, but they quickly become swamped and don't have the skill, power, or infrastructure to say "no" when things get to be too much. Quality starts to suffer, and then doubts start creeping in as to whether or not these are the right people, or whether successful content marketing is even possible.

The Purpose activity, then, is to develop and manage a clear set of core responsibilities and processes that build and continually assess the allocation of resources, skill sets, and clear charters that a content marketing team will need in order to become a differentiated *business* capability. One of those skills may be the actual creation of content—but there are assuredly others as well (and we'll explore them later in this book).

That leads to the second activity category in the Communication pillar: the Model, or content-as-coordinated-communications. The Model activity (covered in Chapter 4) also overlaps into the Operations pillar, which we'll describe shortly.

Every business that succeeds with content marketing strategy will have a well-defined and well-understood governance/operating model. For example, the business we just discussed, with all those journalists, may end up with an entire department devoted to content marketing as a "centralized" team. Cleveland Clinic is a great example of this. The world-renowned hospital has created a centralized content marketing department that is a functioning business unit. They started with a handful of content creators and evolved into a diverse, and multi-functional, but centralized, team with clear and standard operating processes.

Other businesses may deploy a "federated model" in which the content team is responsible for creating only a small percentage of content. In fact, their entire functional model may be devoted to enabling the other departments in the business to create, manage, activate, and measure quality content across multiple channels. Their role—much like a federal government—is really to provide a centralized place where "laws" (e.g., standards, playbooks, workflows, etc.) are created and kept, so that everyone is working in the same way. A great example of this is Anthem Blue Cross Insurance (now Elevance Health). This company employs 98,000 people and consists of multiple businesses including pharmaceutical insurance, dental insurance, long-term care, and disability. You'll read more about their journey in the next chapter, but one of the keys for the content team leader there was to create a formal charter for her team. They created an organizational process where the different product groups have coordinated representation, allowing each to interface with the content team. The brand content team is responsible for curating, creating, packaging, and making available Elevance-level brand stories.

2: *A portfolio of experiences*

You've just learned that a coordinated communication/content approach is managing the quantity, and quality, of what the entire business wants to say. That leads us to the second pillar of a content marketing strategy—Experiences—all the way at the other end of the spectrum. Experiences are the designed containers of content being created for audiences. No matter how big a business is, it needs a strategic approach to how the content it creates will be utilized to power designed platforms such as emails, websites, resource centers, print magazines, PDF files, events, blogs, or even social media channels.

This is a critical aspect of *operating* like a media company that has owned media properties. For example, when a media company thinks of its next production, it may start as a movie, but then almost immediately, operational and management processes kick in to explore how that same content will be leveraged in books, television, podcasts, interactive entertainment, etc. The story comes first, and then the thinking for all the different kinds of containers that might express that story in different ways.

Remember, for media companies the experience that they monetize *is the product*. And they have two primary ways of monetizing it. They monetize access to the experience with models like subscription or selling a limited number of tickets. Or, media companies will monetize the experience by selling access to the audience consuming it by allowing sponsors to create content that will be contained in it. This is the model of advertising, or sponsored content.

Our owned media experiences for business should be no different. All of a brand's owned media channels—the website, blog, resource center, e-commerce catalog, print magazine, etc.—should be treated with the same care and consideration as the existing product/service lines. Just like a media company, we should think "content first," and then how we will create all the different kinds of containers to deliver that content. We manage all of these as a portfolio of experiences that exploit valuable content for audiences. Each container should have strategic purpose, goals, and objectives. Arguing, for example, that our website or our blog is less important than any of our products and services is essentially arguing that they shouldn't exist at all.

So, as with any product or service, someone needs to be responsible for ensuring that these experiences are updated and that they have charters, goals, and specific strategies that are optimized to meet the needs of the consumers (audiences) they serve. They should be designed and evolved to meet new market demands, promoted in a standard way, and measured against shared business goals. Further, like any of our products and services, they should be easily discontinued when they no longer suit our business objectives.

This pillar is founded on the idea that there is a team focused on the process of producing and managing the platforms of a company's owned media strategy in a way that is optimal for the company's business goals.

The two activity categories within this pillar are Audience and Value.

Audience is where the business must define each experience as a product. In other words, Audience is content-as-product. This harkens back to the earliest days of the 4 Ps. Just like we would create a plan for every product or service we would bring to market, we now need to create product plans for our owned media experiences. This means crafting a solution that fits a market need, initiating market research into the audience and understanding them well, and having specific, measurable goals for each content-driven experience being launched. This book dives deep into the Audience activity in Chapter 5.

Treating experiences this way helps us deliver their ultimate goal, which is Value. Value is content-as-insight. Meeting all of the designed objectives of a portfolio of experiences delivers the value of the content marketing strategy. This activity is where we integrate insight and map out exactly where, when, and how the content marketing strategy will provide it. Designing a measurement and value approach is a core piece of Chapter 8 of this book.

And that gets us to the third content marketing strategy pillar, the glue that holds Coordinated Communication and Experiences together.

3: *Strategic operations*

Consider for a moment the practice of accounting. It is one of the oldest business practices in the world, dating back to the 1400s when mathematician Luca Pacioli created the double-entry accounting system and introduced the idea of ledgers, journals, and bookkeeping.

The reasons for standards and predictable guidelines in accounting are easy to understand. Finance touches every part of a business. Everyone in business does some form of accounting, from the way time sheets are completed to procurement requisitions, vendor relationships, product sales, and even the use of raw materials for products and services.

Now think about content and marketing. Today, it is just as pervasive as accounting—or even more so in some cases. Creating content for business communication touches every single part of the business. It's the water in which we swim.

Yet, most businesses handle the creation, management, distribution, and measurement of content in an ad hoc manner.

Remember, it's not just marketing that is changing, it is the entire business strategy. Thus, the CEO's or business owner's relationship with marketing and content changes as well. In a 2022 article for McKinsey Consulting, one former retail CEO said, "Data has changed how the C-suite is interacting with marketing. Now it's very hard to separate company strategy from marketing strategy."[6] If that is true, then it's also true that it's hard to separate company strategy from our content strategy.

Today, marketing departments are looked at as factories—places where something successful should be replicable a million times.

In order to achieve consistency in replicating success and become a core business strategy, content marketing must have a clearly articulated and replicable process that can flex and accommodate new ideas as they emerge. The activity in this pillar is the Frame, or content-as-standard.

If activation of engaging content is now the heart of marketing, content operations are what make the heart beat. Getting content marketing operations right frees creative people to do creative things that enable the business strategy, and empowers the marketing teams to achieve this at scale.

As we've established, everyone in the business creates content: the web team, the marketing automation/demand-gen team, the content marketing team, agencies, executives, frontline account representatives, salespeople, human resources, even accounting with invoices, contracts, and onboarding documentation. In fact, it's probably easier to count all the people who *don't* create digital customer communications these days. We've established that setting up communications coordination is a primary pillar of a standardized approach to content. Additionally, today businesses operate in a multichannel world with, typically, dozens of channels (experiences) that have to be populated with content in multiple formats. For example, consider a company that launches two to four new products each quarter. For each new product launch there are 10 assets planned, including brochures, product tech briefs, a thought leadership paper, etc. That may not sound like very much, but each of the 10 assets needs to be customized for the five major service partners that will support the marketing, and each of those service partners has promotional assets that need to be customized for different content types or channel specifications (social media, video, etc.). Finally, all of those assets need to be translated into four languages. The net result is that 10 planned pieces of content turn into approximately 300 digital assets that need to be designed and produced. Multiply that by two new products per quarter, and you end up with approximately 2,400 digital assets created every year just for new product launches.

So, it doesn't matter how big the business is—a repeatable set of processes must be put in place that are governed by standards, guidelines, playbooks, and technology. We call this the Frame activities, because very much like the frame of your house, it's what holds everything up. It is content-as-a-standard.

This third pillar, Operations, is the people, processes, and technology that help create a repeatable, consistent process to connect the coordinated content creators (Pillar 1) with the experiences powered by the content they are creating (Pillar 2). With the right content operational model in place, you can scale and measure enterprise content.

Together these three pillars and the five building-block activities form a competency framework for the entirety of your content marketing strategy. They are pressure points that help to determine how strong, or weak, your strategy is.

For example, when I work with a company that is struggling with the purpose of their corporate blog, I might first press on the Audience button (which we'll do in Chapter 5). I can see how strong we are at a company-wide understanding of how well we perform that activity. I can examine what makes that category of activity different, or optimal. That, then, helps me as a strategist understand where I may need to change the activity or strengthen any of the other pillars of coordinating communication, operational processes, or managing the experiences.

This framework puts a conceptual structure to meaningful questions that must be answered:

- What competencies and skill sets are needed for different roles of people, process, and technologies in the business in each of the pillars?

- What working models will be required, valued, recognized, and rewarded with regard to a functioning content strategy?

- How will we define the internal processes of operating like a media company, so that this can be scaled and measured as an effective business function?

- How will the framework provide for measurable objectives, the results of which will provide insight into the value being created for both the audiences and the business?

- How do we guide the differentiating operational focus for content marketing that can provide the evolving competitive advantage that the business wants?

You may wonder whether there is an overarching template, a cheatsheet, or standardized answers to these questions. Fortunately, or perhaps unfortunately for those of you who are looking for the quick answer, there is not. Welcome to the art and science of content marketing strategy. It reminds me of the challenge that James Culliton faced in 1948 while introducing the marketing mix, and Jerome McCarthy had in 1960 introducing the 4 Ps. While the framework may be useful, there is no single answer for any one company about a template marketing mix or use of the 4 Ps. The ingredients for your perfect mix of content marketing strategy will be yours, and will be very different.

There is no template. There is no perfect recipe.

One of the most important things we've learned after working on content marketing strategy for hundreds of brands over the last decade is that what you put into those categories of activities is much less important than consciously making the decision to put something in there.

Just as there is no perfect marketing mix, there is no perfect content marketing strategy. You will evolve. It will change. Because you and your business will change.

As statistician George Box once said, "All models are wrong, but some are useful."[7]

Successful content marketing, either consciously or unconsciously, uses elements of this model to bolster its operation. As I said at the beginning, the successful, happy content marketers seem to have a similar way of working.

This is a model that we've seen work—it's been tested. In fact, you may have realized at some point during this chapter that the rest of this book is organized by covering each of the categories of activities in our content marketing strategy model. If you can formulate, structure, and pressure-test your activities in each box, then you are well on your way to creating a great content marketing strategy.

Now that you know the structure, we'll dig into the first box in the next chapter: Purpose.

Let's get to it.

Notes

1 Culliton, J. (1948) *The Management of Marketing Costs*, 1st ed, Andover, MA: Andover Press, p.6

2 McCarthy, E.J. (1960) *Basic Marketing: A managerial approach*, 1st ed, Richard D. Irwin, Inc, p.51

3 Pulizzi, J. and Rose, R. (2018b) *Killing Marketing: How innovative businesses are turning marketing cost into profit*, New York: McGraw-Hill Education, p.36

4 Jones, B. (2015) Arrow buys Hearst's technical media assets—who'll buy UBM's?, Publitek, www.publitek.com/news/arrow-buys-hearsts-technical-media-assets-wholl-buy-ubms/ (archived at https://perma.cc/NYU8-FQFX)

5 Avery, G. (2016) Arrow Electronics buying UBM's EE Times, other tech publications, Bizjournals.com, www.bizjournals.com/denver/blog/boosters_bits/2016/06/arrow-electronics-buying-ubms-ee-times-other-tech.html (archived at https://perma.cc/6XF8-RX2U)

6 Cvetanovski, B. (2019) Views from the top: What CEOs and other execs really think of marketing, McKinsey, www.mckinsey.com/capabilities/growth-marketing-and-sales/our-insights/views-from-the-top-what-ceos-and-other-execs-really-think-of-marketing (archived at https://perma.cc/84EE-5XC7)

7 Box, G. (1976) Science and Statistics, *Journal of the American Statistical Association*, 71(356), pp.791–9, http://www-sop.inria.fr/members/Ian.Jermyn/philosophy/writings/Boxonmaths.pdf (archived at https://perma.cc/27UZ-XDK5)

Designing a Strategic Purpose

03

Assembling Teams, Charters, and Clear Responsibilities

Everybody in business loves innovation and change. You know, just so long as it doesn't affect them.

Now that we have a framework, let's begin with designing our strategy with a purpose.

Whose responsibility is content marketing strategy—and what will it accomplish?

You might have looked at the three pillars and five categories and thought, "This looks overwhelming." Maybe you pressed (mentally) on each of those five categories, and you concluded, "I just don't know. Maybe they're broken. But maybe they're not."

I know. Frustrating.

Content marketing strategy is a wicked problem.

Now, don't worry. I didn't just suddenly adopt Bostonian slang. A "wicked problem" is something that comes from social policy planning. It is a problem that is hard to solve because of "incomplete, contradictory, or changing requirements that can be difficult to recognize."

Information researcher Jeff Conklin described wicked problems as those "not understood until after the formulation of a solution."[1] Put simply: It's sometimes hard to understand the scope of a problem until after you've tried solving it a few times.

In my consulting work, I see wicked problems a lot in mapping out a content marketing strategy. Why? Because it usually involves changing something that isn't seen as fundamentally broken. It's difficult to create a vision for how you need to change roles and responsibilities for people when you can't really see how (or if) things are broken, or how challenges will be improved if they're fixed.

Here's an example. My wife and I get around our kitchen just fine. We cook. The kitchen gets messy. We clean up and put things back where they go. We do the same thing at the next meal. It works okay for us. While we both would acknowledge it's probably not an ideal process, we see no problems that require solving.

Recently, a friend who came over for dinner wanted to help us cook. It was pure chaos. "Nothing is in the right place," our guest said. She went to our junk drawer looking for cutlery and opened our spice cabinet seeking plates. "Don't even get me started with how the refrigerator is organized," she said.

My wife responded, "This is how we've been doing this for years. It works for us." Then I chimed in, "It's the way we do it. It's an optimized process."

Our friend played along and said, "No. It's the way *you* do it. But it's not optimized."

She was right. As she pointed out how a few things could be changed to be more effective, and efficient, we finally understood we had a problem that was worth solving.

Wicked.

In my consulting work in content marketing strategy, one of the biggest challenges I tend to observe in most companies is not a lack of creative ideas, bad content, poorly implemented technology, or even misplaced objectives. No. Usually, the biggest challenge is simply a lack of any kind of conscious responsibility, charter, or even knowledge about who is responsible for making the decisions about what content is created, when it's created, how much of a priority it is, where it should go, and how it will be utilized once it's created.

There's no purpose there. And without a purpose it's really hard to fix, well, nothing.

It sounds crazy given how much content is created by most businesses. But if you ask most people in most businesses how all their content is created, they'll mostly just shrug and say, "We create it. Content just… happens. It just works."

As my friend might say, "That's the way *you* do it. But it's definitely not optimized."

But, okay, if it's working, why do we care about optimizing it?

Don't ship the org chart

At the beginning of this book, I discussed how senior leadership was probably already annoyed that marketers haven't done more with content. I suggested that we not go to the CEO with a new type of approach to marketing, but rather a more organized and purposeful way of performing the activities of content. That's a content marketing strategy.

However, we need to be thoughtful about how we approach this conversation with our boss, or our colleagues. If we simply push for a team responsible for and dedicated to the consistent process of creating quality content as its purpose, the kneejerk pushback from senior leadership in business to this problem is to ask, "Well, is that really a problem?" Is content getting created? Yes. Is the content working to engage audiences and acquire customers? Sometimes, yes. "So," says the senior leader, "if we are already doing it, why do we need a team dedicated to it? Why don't we just assume that we have some means of creating content—a 'content factory' if you will—and worry more about the quality of the widgets coming out of it, instead of how it gets made?"

Well, as it turns out, Steven Sinofsky has a great answer to that question. Steven is a product marketing guru and former president of the Windows division at Microsoft. He is most famous for saying "Don't ship the org chart."[2]

It's great advice. Make sure what you're offering—whether it's software like Windows, a product like a phone, a consulting service, or even something less tangible like content and customer experiences—is built to satisfy customer needs and desires instead of reflecting your internal organizational structure, your silos, your turf battles, your budget constraints. It just makes sense.

For example, have you ever dealt with a customer service representative at a large company and they have to "transfer you to another department"—or worse, give you a different 1-800 number to call—in order to facilitate the specific help you require? That's shipping the org chart.

A content marketing example of shipping the org chart is when your prospective customer registers for your amazing email newsletter and continues to enjoy it for a couple of months, learning in-depth from your expertise. But then, one day, when they email a response to that newsletter and ask to speak with someone who might help them purchase, they get an automated response from the business informing them that if they're interested in speaking with sales, to phone this number. Or, if they wish to speak with customer service, they should email this particular address. Or, if they have a question, they can review the FAQ on the website. And, if and when a salesperson finally does reach out, the potential customer is treated as if they have no idea about what the company does, or how it goes to market. It's as if sales have no idea that the customer has been learning and engaging with your brand for months.

Because they don't.

At the surface, Steven's warning—"Don't ship the org chart"—is often taken as a warning that we should be aware of the experience we're creating and run it through some kind of "quality check" to ensure it doesn't reflect those organizational silos.

But, as it turns out, when Steven says "Don't ship the org chart," he doesn't mean that you shouldn't ship the org chart. In fact, he means the opposite. It's not a warning about something to avoid. It is a statement of fact about something that is, well, unavoidable. You *will* ship the org chart. Every. Time.

It is inevitable. Inescapable. Pre-ordained. And, in fact, Steven was deliberately invoking what's called Conway's law, an observation made by Melvin Conway, a computer scientist and developer. In 1968 he noted: "Organizations that design systems… are constrained to produce designs which are copies of the communication structures of these organizations."[3]

In other words, your organizational design *is intrinsic* to your communication. And, remember, for our purposes content = communication.

So the way we treat the organizational design for content *is intrinsic* to how effectively we will communicate.

As both Steven and Melvin teach: Since we inevitably communicate in the way we are organized, you better organize and operate in the way you want to communicate to customers.

So, our goal to establish purpose is not to push for a team that is responsible and dedicated to the consistent process of creating quality content. It is, rather, to organize a charter, clarify roles and responsibilities, and establish content marketing so as to establish a coordinated purpose of how we want the business to communicate.

The answer to the pushback of someone asking whether organizing a charter or clarifying roles and responsibilities for content marketing strategy is useful is to ask: Do we want to communicate in the most optimal way possible?

Spoiler alert: If the answer to that question isn't a resounding "Yes," then we have other issues.

Our content will always reflect our internal structures, our strengths and weaknesses across those different teams, and the different approaches that each takes. So, this wicked problem is worth solving. But how do we decide?

Creating team purpose and a charter for that purpose

There's a quote by a great philosopher—Uncle Ben from the Spider-Man franchise—that says, "With great power comes great responsibility." These are wise words from Uncle Ben and are rarely heeded, which is why they are so powerful to a young Peter Parker as he grapples with his newfound superpowers as Spider-Man.

Many have taken that idea and used it to assume that the inverse is also true: *With great responsibility comes great power*. Now, this inversion may be technically true when we are in self-reflection, but my experience is that in this case we are not truly inverting the idea. We're actually just fully processing the first way of saying it. We realize that fully taking responsibility for our own choices is actually a superpower, but that expressing that superpower requires that we do so judiciously and responsibly.

In business—and especially marketing—I find the inverse to be exceedingly rare. We almost never see someone step up, take responsibility for an innovative or new activity, and then automatically receive the granted power of control over that new activity. As I've said before, everybody in business loves innovation and change—you know, as long as it works.

This is why when any business executive asks me what the very first and most important step in creating a content marketing strategy is, I say, "It is both making someone (or a team) responsible for it, and then consciously acknowledging their power to manage it."

For example, in 2021, my consulting firm had the pleasure of working with Elevance Health, formerly known as Anthem Insurance. The company is the largest Blue Cross Blue Shield for-profit healthcare company in the United States. As of 2022, the company had more than 46 million customers within their multiple affiliated health plans.

As the company planned to completely re-brand from Anthem to Elevance Health, one of the biggest parts of the initiative was to reintroduce the company to customers and unify their family of brands to reflect a transition from an insurance company to a health company.

Jennifer Hovelsrud was a new hire as a Staff Vice President of Enterprise Content Marketing Strategy. She saw an opportunity to create new content strategy and processes to help tell the company's new story more broadly, more efficiently, and in a more effective way. In short: She envisioned customer-centric brand experiences across a number of channels (including web, social, and other more traditional media). She saw it as an opportunity to have great content marketing make a meaningful contribution to unifying and differentiating the new brand as not just another insurance company, but one ready, willing, and able to do great things for the world.

Her goals were to bring more awareness to other very specific company solutions in disparate markets, but to provide a more central brand consistency and story across these areas. With every product/service group running its own marketing and brand strategy, along with intricacies, complexities, and regulations of different insurance marketplaces in a $44 billion organization, this was no small task.

So what did Jennifer do?

She took on the responsibility and built what she called an "enterprise thought leadership framework and strategy" that would connect what the brand said to their actions. This was both a specifically defined charter and operational model for her team and a proposed framework for all the creative leadership themes across all of those disparate solutions. As Gandhi might say, Jennifer had her team become the change she wished to see communicated from the organization. She created a purpose.

Then, and most importantly, she brought together leaders from around the organization to form an "editorial council" to help bring the thought leadership framework to life and begin to get "buy-in" for accepting the responsibility to centralize this brand story and mission across the broader enterprise.

She then refined a formal charter for her team, and a proposed organizational process where the different product groups would have representation, allowing each to interface with Jennifer's brand content team. Her brand content team has responsibility for curating, creating, packaging, and making available Elevance-level brand stories, which can then be utilized by the more niche business units in their markets. Further, the brand content team created the standards, guidelines, and playbooks for how content should be originated by these product teams.

One of the most critical aspects of the successful launch of this initiative was how the CMO and CEO approved making Jennifer's content marketing team "official" so that it would be recognized company-wide. They were not only provided the responsibility of creating a content marketing strategy, they were afforded the requisite power to manage a coordinated and consistent strategy that would be recognized as such.

As Jennifer said to me in a recent interview:

> We all know that just having a content marketing strategy alone will not change perceptions in the marketplace. You have to enable the

entire organization to speak consistently and in a way that ensures cohesive storytelling. The key for making this work was not only our ability to create a central framework for thought leadership and brand storytelling, but the clear charter and empowerment we were given by senior leadership to execute against it. Content isn't strategic until the entire business acknowledges that it is.[4]

With Jennifer's story in mind, let's walk through the first steps of defining a purpose and team charter for our content marketing strategy.

Defining the responsibilities in the content lifecycle

In Chapter 2 we discussed the three core pillars of content marketing strategy. Much like the 4 Ps of marketing, these three pillars contain the sum of all activities that will be performed as part of a content marketing approach.

So, the first thing we need to do within the Purpose category is to define the core activities (or responsibilities) that are within these pillars. In the simplest of terms, how will we manage the "content lifecycle" from ideation all the way through to measurement? This is going to help us understand this "wicked problem."

When we think about how we're going to allocate all of our time, resources, etc., we like to categorize things. In our personal lives, those categories might be work, lifestyle, family. In our business lives, they might be via divisions, marketing, sales, product, human resources, accounting, etc.

In order to make a plan for how we will accommodate all the activities that need to be performed as part of our content marketing strategy, we first need to identify what they are—categorize them.

Within each of the three pillars, a six-step lifecycle for content makes up the categories of responsibilities that need to be applied. But now we can see how the three pillars of content align with a very linear content lifecycle process. As you can see in Figure 3.1, each of the six responsibilities flows through the three pillars from

Figure 3.1 The Six Responsibilities Aligned With the Three Pillars

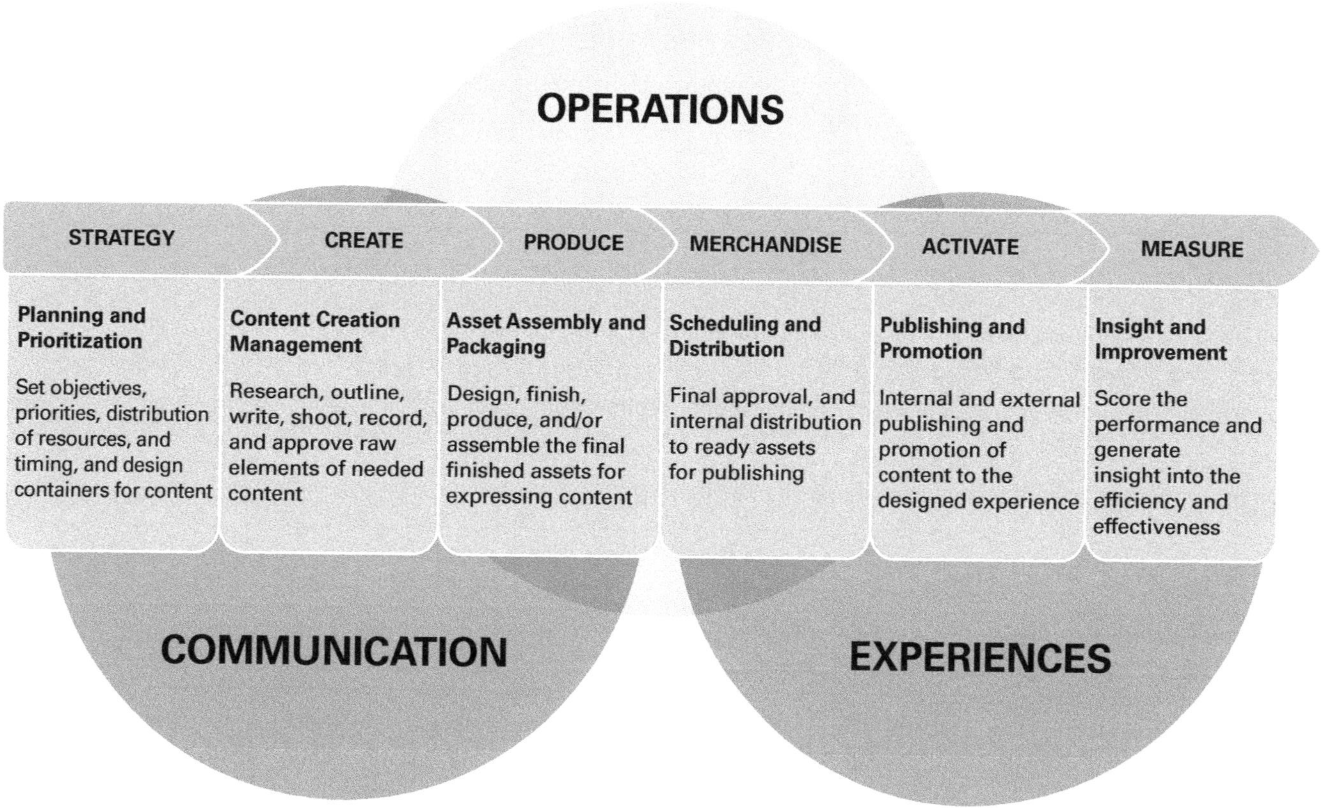

	STRATEGY	CREATE	PRODUCE	MERCHANDISE	ACTIVATE	MEASURE
	Planning and Prioritization	**Content Creation Management**	**Asset Assembly and Packaging**	**Scheduling and Distribution**	**Publishing and Promotion**	**Insight and Improvement**
	Set objectives, priorities, distribution of resources, and timing, and design containers for content	Research, outline, write, shoot, record, and approve raw elements of needed content	Design, finish, produce, and/or assemble the final finished assets for expressing content	Final approval, and internal distribution to ready assets for publishing	Internal and external publishing and promotion of content to the designed experience	Score the performance and generate insight into the efficiency and effectiveness

OPERATIONS

EXPERIENCES

COMMUNICATION

NOTE There is a six-step lifecycle for content that runs from ideation and planning through to measurement and insight. They generally align with the three pillars and the strategic function of content. At each step, there are responsibilities that need to be assigned, and clarified.

coordination of content, through operations, and ultimately into our portfolio of experiences.

And, of course, our new content team won't be responsible for all of them across all three pillars. So, we start by defining them (and what we will and won't be responsible for) as our Purpose—within the Content Coordination pillar. The six responsibility categories are:

1 Strategy: Planning and Prioritization

As with any communication, strategic content is planned and prioritized. Not all ideas for content are good, and most should be combined with others. So a key first step in the content lifecycle is a coordinated activity of cross-functional planning, resource allotment, and prioritization for content.

2 Create: Content Assembly and Editing

One of the biggest challenges in the content lifecycle is separating the idea of content creation (the raw content) and production of the designed assets (the containers). But this is a necessary split to ensure that great content can be repackaged and reused across multiple layouts and designs.

3 Produce: Design and Production

Once content has been created and production gets underway, you must have a planning process to manage that work. This is the activity of designing and producing all of the containers for content that need to be created.

4 Merchandise: Scheduling and Distribution

Think of this as internal distribution of the content produced. If you have planned well, you are creating lots of assets from big ideas, and your publishing schedule looks forward, not behind. In other words, because you've been planning, you're likely completing assets that may not be published for weeks or even months. This responsibility is the internal distribution planning and lifecycle.

5 Activate: Publishing and Promotion

Whether you're a team of one or 100, you should develop activation plans as part of your content plan. After content is published, this is a question of not only a "marketing plan" but of all the content and assets that may need to be created as part of a marketing plan of other content assets.

6 Measure: Analytics and Insight

Who is wrangling and working the decision-making process for *how* you will determine measurement? It's about creating a planning and ongoing management process. Who is responsible for tracking the metrics? Who is accountable for getting the numbers? Who will be consulted? Who needs to be informed about them?

So, with these responsibilities in mind, the question then becomes how you delegate (or assume) each of these six responsibilities across each of the three different pillars. Is one team handling all of the responsibilities across all three pillars, or are multiple teams handling some of the responsibilities and outsourced agencies handling others? Or are all teams handling all of the responsibilities as separate silos?

It's a decision to make. There is no right one. And don't worry—you are building to change, so as things evolve, you may decide to change from one to another. The critical thing is to make a conscious decision about each. Remember, these are activities that you will constantly manage, not projects that cannot be undone.

Defining the charters in content marketing strategy

Once a business acknowledges this lifecycle, and where the responsibilities will lie across the different areas, the first step to making it real is defining the purpose of the people who will be responsible for making it so. This is more than just getting "buy-in" or "permission" for a team to take on responsibilities for existing activities. It means that the organization must recognize that, based on a specific purpose, there will be different activities, and special skills needed, and thus the roles that will be created are specific to a content marketing strategy.

Remember what Jen from Elevance Health did. She *first* created the functional thought leadership framework, the themes, and the operational charter for how content marketing strategy should work. She created the purpose of how the organization would communicate. Then she made that an extension of how she went out to get buy-in. Remember, she *became the change* she wanted to see. She knew she would ship the org chart, so she created the purpose first, so that changes to the org would communicate in a way that supported that purpose.

What Jen did NOT do was to architect some hypothetical proposal in a PowerPoint deck, and then go seek permission to be empowered to create this thing. In other words, Jen built the lighthouse and then went to management to get buy-in on making it the official standard for directing the ships.

But, regardless of whether we are changing institutional processes in a large company like Elevance, or creating a brand-new functional team in a small company, or something in between, I know you're left with a big question at this point:

Where should *we* start?

- What roles and responsibilities should this content team take on?
- What is the overarching operating model for the content marketing strategy?
- What's the right way for us to build this?

We have found that the best place to start is with a self-assessment of the best overall charter for your content marketing strategy.

Whenever we see content marketing strategy succeeding, we can trace the success to a clear charter for the person (or team) in charge of it. One successful way of determining what a starting charter should be for your content marketing strategy team is to do an assessment of where the focus should be today, and where you might want to evolve to tomorrow.

We developed a model for examining this focus.

A self-assessment for your team's charter and purpose

At this point, you can see the six categories of responsibilities aligned across the three pillars and, hopefully, you can start to see that each of the six will contain activities that need to "fit together" in order for us to express our strategy.

But, how do you make these decisions? What tools can help you prioritize which activities should be taken by your team versus delegated to others in our business?

In other words, you have the puzzle pieces, but what is the picture (the purpose) that is formed by putting them together? I have found that the best way to get there is to paint the current picture (where you are today) and then envision our ideal picture for tomorrow (the future). This will give you an overall vision. This is where you can use a bit of a self-assessment to help you understand where you are today (if anywhere) and where you might want to go in the future.

A tool that can help us sketch out this future is a purpose-driven canvas that can help us get directional clarity on which responsibilities—and thus charters—we should focus on (if only at first).

So, in the model in Figure 3.2, you can see that there are four quadrants along two axes. On the Y axis are charters that are internally focused versus more externally focused.

Figure 3.2   A Functional Purpose-Driven Canvas

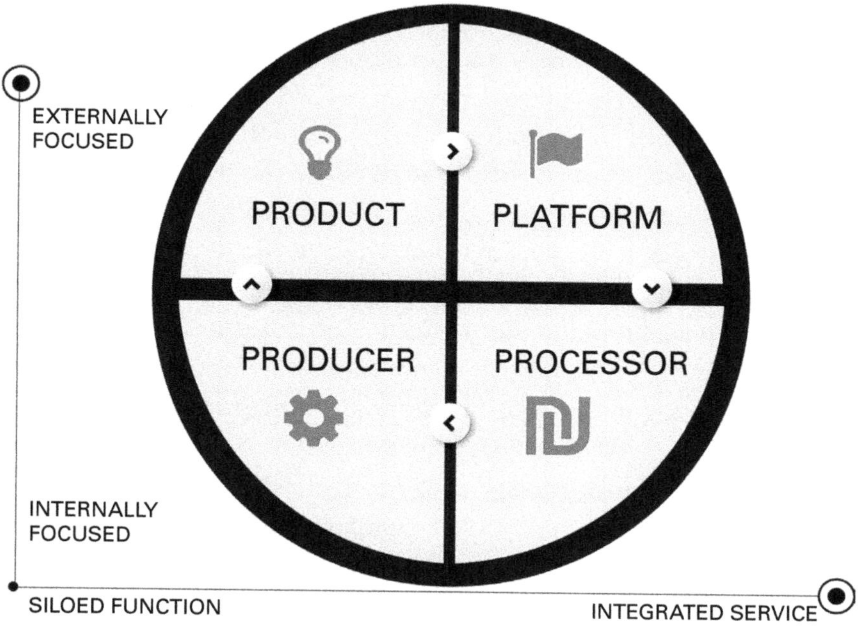

NOTE Plotting where our current purpose is, and where we may want to shift (or create) over time, can help us get directional clarity on which responsibilities, and thus charters, we should focus on first.

In other words, at the lower end of this spectrum are teams who are destined to serve as an internal service function; their purpose is to produce content that will be used by other marketing and sales teams across the business—the internal "content factory," if you will. There is nothing inherently wrong with this charter, but there are specific responsibilities, powers, and processes that go along with it. So, instead of defaulting there, the business should make a conscious choice for it.

Now, this is not binary. So as we plot toward the upper end of this axis, the purpose of the team becomes more *externally* focused: More of a media operation assembled with a purpose to separately build and manage content experiences for audiences that can be monetized by the business over time.

As an example, at the lowest end of that spectrum, think of the "internal agency" model—where the purpose is to ideate, plan, and deliver content to demand generation teams, sales teams, and perhaps others to drive more traditional (and efficient) marketing campaigns. Then, at the upper end of that spectrum, think of a dedicated editorial team, with a chartered purpose of managing a strategic digital experience (like a blog, resource center, email newsletter, or others) that drives subscribed audiences and leverages them for marketing purposes. And, of course, in between the two extremes are teams that would be balanced to do both to varying degrees.

Then, along the X axis at the bottom of the model, we see charters on the left that are departmental (e.g., siloed) services. At the extreme left it might be simply a team whose dedicated purpose is to serve only one particular function (say, PR or sales enablement) with one singular responsibility (creation, production, measurement, etc.). But then, as we move right, it evolves into more fully integrated business services, handling multiples of the responsibilities to multiple areas of the business.

For example, Laura Barnes is the Senior Director, Global Content Team at Red Hat Linux, an IBM company and one of the leading providers of open-source software. Laura's team started eight years ago squarely on the left-hand side of this spectrum: siloed and providing only one kind of content marketing for the product marketing team. Today, her dynamic team of 50 now provides all kinds of content across the entire enterprise, including podcasts, email newsletters, and community. Additionally, the team provides strategic services such as UI/UX development, governance, SEO, and other enterprise content services.[5]

Four quadrants to help us paint a picture

Ultimately, this gives us four broad quadrants—or foundational purposes—of operating charters to start our content marketing strategy. Each is a spectrum, of course, but by identifying where we fall today, and where we want to go by plotting our goals across the four, we can begin to more easily determine what the right charter is for our particular team.

The quick and easy way to explain and think about each of these four models is to look at the output they typically produce.

We begin in the lower left with the Producer Purpose. As I've stated throughout this book, this is certainly the most common for existing companies. This is often one, two, or three people—although it can be many more—who are tasked with fulfilling the content marketing needs of the business by creating, producing, and merchandising content marketing assets (the "content factory"). This is a dedicated team whose purpose is to serve the internal constituencies with communication. This team produces the infographics, ebooks, and sales sheets, populates the blog on the website, and often creates thought leadership presentations for the CEO.

When this team is functional and strategic, they are seen as a strategic internal resource—an internal agency. They are considered a group of people who can be counted on to lead and produce great content for business purposes. At the extreme lower left, it might be one small team focused only on producing content marketing for one team. As it stretches toward the middle right, it might be an internal content studio charged with creating and managing content marketing assets for many areas of the business.

When this purpose is dysfunctional, it can often be seen as the vending machine of content. They are the company's version of a neighborhood Kinkos, where you put in your "order" for content and hope that good stuff comes out the other side. This is where you can "press" on the purpose and start to understand where there may be opportunities to change.

That gets us to the lower right-hand quadrant: the Processor Purpose. This is again an internally focused team, but leans toward providing more integrated business services that the whole enterprise uses. Maybe the business has a team or teams not only providing content, but also providing SEO strategy or perhaps translation, localization, analytics, or best practices governance guidelines. This charter also means that (because there are more integrated services being provided) it should also be setting business standards for how content will be created, managed, and measured, whether in the organization or by outsourced agencies.

Then, as we move up to the upper left, we have the Product Purpose. Here in the extreme upper left, the focus of the content marketing strategy is on building external audiences, but only for one departmental purpose. There may be an editorial team managing a resource center or a dedicated blog or a magazine or video channel—discrete, immersive experiences aimed at nurturing audiences. As we move to the right, this team's purpose becomes to manage multiple experiences that serve many parts of the business. This charter is all about how to use a content marketing strategy to build owned media experiences to attract and retain audiences.

Then, finally, in the upper right, we have the Platform charter. The purpose here is as an integrated business strategy, where content is not only being created as a marketing and sales tactic, but maybe even as an integrated product or monetized business strategy. This is where the content marketing strategy is an ingrained part of the overall business strategy—and there may even be monetized platforms that draw revenue in addition to serving as marketing and communications platforms.

I spoke earlier of Cleveland Clinic and its success as a centralized content marketing strategy. Cleveland Clinic isn't just a local hospital; it is a massive global health system with 21 hospitals and an operating revenue of more than $12 billion.

Amanda Todorovich, Cleveland Clinic's Executive Director for Content Marketing, started her journey at the company with an operation that was squarely in the lower left-hand side of the model. In 2012, her team was three people who tracked content demands from people across the organization on spreadsheets, and served mostly to manage the social media channels.

Today, the team is more than 100, and is made up of everything from editors, writers, SEO experts, video production, email and podcast producers to data scientists. *Health Essentials*, Cleveland Clinic's main digital publication, brings in more than 12 million visits every month, and enough meaningful revenue to the company that the team now also includes sales and audience development managers. They are operating exactly like a media company.

It's a balance of activities, not a maturity model

Now, it's very tempting to look at the four charters as a maturity scale or a state, where you start with baby steps with only the Producer charter and expand the strategic purpose (and resources) of the team to grow up and to the right into becoming a Platform content team.

While there are elements of truth to this (e.g., most businesses almost always start out in the Producer model and more sophisticated content marketing strategies lean heavily toward a Platform charter), it's misleading to see these as stages or levels of maturity.

Most successful, and strategic, content marketing charters are simply a balanced combination of all four approaches that address whatever the business objectives are. Many larger businesses in fact have multiple teams that tackle specific purposes. So it's not a question of which one are we now and how do we grow up and to the right as quickly as possible. Rather, an intelligent content marketing strategy is about identifying what balance of all four we are today, and asking what balance of the four makes the most sense for the business tomorrow.

For example, as you can see in Figure 3.3, a balanced charter may start by focusing on being a Producer of content as its primary purpose.

Figure 3.3   The Balanced Canvas

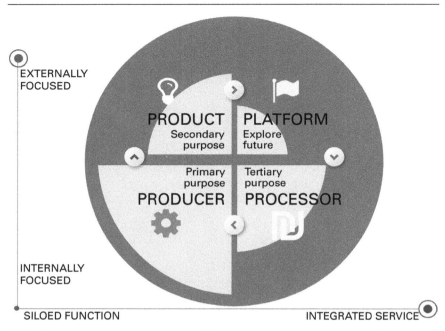

NOTE A balanced strategy may mean we initially focus on one primary purpose, and also have some participation in and responsibility for others, while we save one for future exploration.

However, it may have a smaller, secondary purpose: To manage a corporate blog. Then, it may have a tertiary purpose to provide supporting services such as SEO, translation, or persona development across the entirety of the business. In this structure, there may be another complete team (or external agency) that focuses on providing these services across the business—but the content team's charter is simply to influence a small part of those services. Finally, this team may identify that its future endeavor is to explore some of the platform-oriented infrastructures (perhaps for the corporate blog that it's managing).

The key insight is that focus in each of the four purpose-driven charters requires different skill sets, roles, responsibilities, and measurement approaches across the three pillars of our content marketing strategy. So, the initial task is to do a self-assessment and determine both "what should be" today and "what may be" tomorrow. In other words, plot out the right kind of model for you.

As I told you in the beginning: More questions. Not answers. In other words, you might decide, "Well, we have a particular set of skills today, and so we should balance our efforts here for now." Or you may decide that you have desires to construct against a particular purpose (as Jen at Elevance Health did), so you're trying to identify the skills you need to grow into.

Too often, where we see businesses struggle with scaling and measuring content marketing, it is because their purpose (if they have one) is completely out of balance with the capabilities of the team.

This self-assessment tool is a high-level tool that can help identify the three most common imbalances, with suggestions for steps you can take to address the challenges they pose.

Would you like to take the self-assessment for your organization and see a sample team purpose charter? We have it available exclusively for readers of this book at ContentMarketingStrategy.com

Think new, not change

Now that we have developed our charter, the responsibilities we want our team to take, remember: Now we need to ensure that we have the power. How do we get the business to recognize our new proposed change?

Remember, everybody loves success. Nobody likes to change.

Clayton Christensen, author of *The Innovator's Dilemma*, wrote about this almost two decades ago. He argued that when a company (or team) matures, there are three areas that affect its capacity to handle a purposeful change: resources, processes, and values.[6]

Christensen suggests that when business teams start with the question "What should (or can) we do?," they always look first at resources, both tangible (people, equipment, and technologies) and less tangible (ideas, designs, and brands).

That makes sense. It's exceedingly rare that our boss comes in and says, "Hey, here's a big audacious goal, just tell me what you need to get there."

If we're lucky, we can start with our existing resources, and success takes root. Then, the business must scale these resources, so it creates processes—codified means of interacting, communicating, and making decisions. Processes make activities more efficient and repeatable. These processes become ingrained and get associated with the company's values.

That makes sense too—and as we'll discover in the next chapter, processes can both be designed and (like that well-worn dirt path that is adjacent to the sidewalk) emerge organically from habit.

Finally, Christensen said, once team members "follow processes and decide priorities by assumption rather than by conscious choice, those processes and values come to constitute the organization's culture."

This gets us all the way back to the wickedness of the problem of content marketing strategy. The biggest thing in our way is the "this is the way we've always done it" mentality around content.

This is why change in business is so darn difficult. Once culture is established, it's virtually impossible to change. As Christensen wrote, "Despite beliefs spawned by popular change-management and reengineering programs, processes are not nearly as flexible or adaptable as resources are."[7]

So, this conclusion provides a way forward for us as we start to put our new charter and purpose into action. Don't try to change the culture by disrupting processes and access to existing resources.

If you want to change the culture around content marketing, you have to begin to create a NEW culture from scratch.

Remember Jen from Elevance Health. She had people at the beginning of her journey (resources). She didn't then go around to every functional area of the business and try to change their culture. Instead, she created a shiny new set of responsibilities (her charter), a new purpose for content (her first projects), and a standards-based approach to content marketing that they could choose to adopt. Then, she went out and socialized.

I see this time and again with our clients' implementation of new content marketing teams and strategy. Consider a company that once told me it tried to create a new content marketing function in its existing business. As initially planned, the existing digital and PR teams would launch new content platforms to build audiences.

But the firm's existing processes and values supported only the idea of centering all digital efforts on its website and using paid and earned media to drive more eyeballs to the website. Ultimately, it wasn't until the company created a *new* "content innovation team" with access to *new* resources, and the creation of *new* processes, that *new* values began to form. They didn't change the existing culture. They created a new one.

There are really only three ways to drive disruptive change for your new charter and approach.

1 Create a new team within your existing business, in which new processes can be built.

2 Spin an existing team out of your organization and give it the ability to create new processes and values.

3 Acquire a different team, whose processes and values are different but aligned with your business goals.

As you start to assemble your team's charter and align against the four models for your initial strategy, remember that it's likely that all four models need to be represented at balanced levels. And it's probably also true that if you were to draw the perfect model for your business, there's a very high likelihood that you wouldn't have the people or resources that you need today.

All of the models have different workflows, resource needs, measurement structures, and methods to scale. This is the real benefit of understanding the balance.

Remember, you can't stop "shipping the org chart." You have to design an org chart that you want to ship.

Notes

1 Wikipedia Contributors (2018) Wicked problem, https://en.wikipedia.org/wiki/Wicked_problem (archived at https://perma.cc/R2EL-WF8U)

2 Sinofsky, S. (2023) Functional versus unit organizations, *Medium*, https://medium.learningbyshipping.com/functional-versus-unit-organizations-6b82bfbaa57 (archived at https://perma.cc/F32W-LKKG)

3 Wikipedia Contributors (2020) Conway's law, https://en.wikipedia.org/wiki/Conway%27s_law (archived at https://perma.cc/3Q65-EXSN)

4 Interview with Jennifer Hovelsrud conducted by Robert Rose, December 12, 2022

5 Johnson, C. (2019) Content leader takes team from lonely silo to powerful presence, Content Marketing Institute, https://contentmarketinginstitute.com/articles/content-team-powerful/ (archived at https://perma.cc/D4XK-E4KJ)

6 Christensen, C.M. and Kaufman, S.P. (2019) Assessing your organization's capabilities: Resources, processes and priorities, Hbs.edu, www.hbs.edu/faculty/Pages/item.aspx?num=33501 (archived at https://perma.cc/SF5Q-QTZP)

7 Christensen, C.M. and Overdorf, M. (2000) Meeting the challenge of disruptive change, *Harvard Business Review*, https://hbr.org/2000/03/meeting-the-challenge-of-disruptive-change (archived at https://perma.cc/VS6C-HKBN)

The Content Marketing Operating Model 04

Building a Governance Frame, Process, and Repeatable Approach

The content marketing team's job is not to be good at content. It is to help the business be good at content.

"I really want to talk about governance," said no one ever.

Don't let the title of this chapter sway you into skipping it. Trust me, I know you want to. You see that word "governance" and you think, "We don't need governance. That's too big for us. We're only a handful of people." Or, "Governance? That sounds like it's above my pay grade." Or, you may think, "Governance? That sounds really boring." You may be right about all of them. Many of the changes and authority required to install a good content marketing strategy may be out of your control. Governance may also not be the sexiest of topics. But that doesn't mean you are powerless, and it doesn't mean it's any less important. You must at least be conscious of it.

Let's tackle this!

As discussed in the previous chapter, a new content marketing team brings people together with a purpose and new responsibilities. As we also discussed, people usually call this process of getting everyone ready for the new situation "change management." But, if we're honest, and we follow Clayton Christensen's teaching, it's really "*new* management." None of this stuff has probably ever been done before.

In the last chapter, we discussed the six responsibilities of content marketing, and how it also aligns with the lifecycle of how we create and use it.

Figure 4.1 The Content Lifecycle Responsibilities

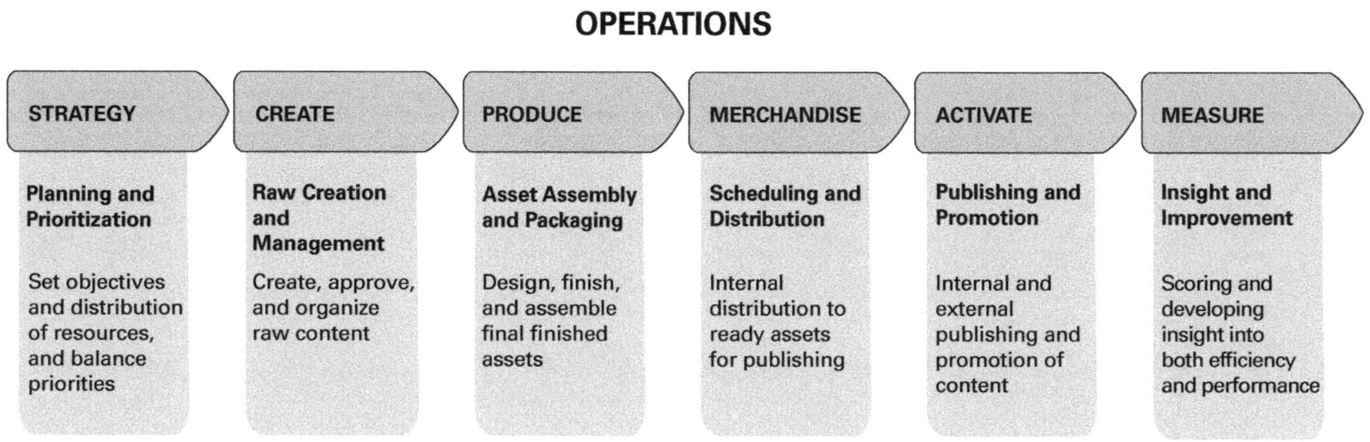

OPERATIONS

STRATEGY	CREATE	PRODUCE	MERCHANDISE	ACTIVATE	MEASURE
Planning and Prioritization	**Raw Creation and Management**	**Asset Assembly and Packaging**	**Scheduling and Distribution**	**Publishing and Promotion**	**Insight and Improvement**
Set objectives and distribution of resources, and balance priorities	Create, approve, and organize raw content	Design, finish, and assemble final finished assets	Internal distribution to ready assets for publishing	Internal and external publishing and promotion of content	Scoring and developing insight into both efficiency and performance

NOTE These six steps across the content lifecycle represent the categories of responsibilities that make up our strategic activities.

The biggest problem with the six responsibilities in this content life-cycle is that while they are perfectly clear, and we've done each one of them from time to time, we don't do each consistently, for all content, or repeatedly in order. And, if now, the new team has said "yes" to any number of them to focus on a purpose and charter, then implicitly, or explicitly, it has also said "no" to others. Put simply: We need to all agree on who is doing what, otherwise we've changed nothing.

Responsibilities are meaningless unless they are coordinated in a way that makes them all into a repeatable and scalable process. That seems kind of obvious, and yet so many businesses fail to apply any process or governance to content. This is the "I don't know how content happens—it just kind of happens" atmosphere that most marketing departments are in. Because content is so pervasive, and it's something everybody does (and in most cases likes to do), it can seem weird to try and put a process around it. The net result is that content becomes everybody's job and no one's strategy.

An unfortunate—but vitally important—task lies before us. In order to create a content marketing strategy, businesses not only have to get their arms around the activities for content marketing but they must also understand how all marketing content is made—full stop.

Chapter 1 showed that content is the water the business swims in. Content is communication. Content *expresses* a business's strategy—it's the byproduct of any and all functions (whether that be brand value, lead generation, sales enablement, customer service, or internal knowledge management initiatives).

Yet, in many businesses, teams in different functions like sales or customer service approach their content needs in a self-centered way. It's not that they are selfish people, it's that content responsibilities have never been made an integrated process, so everyone lacks awareness of the greater context within which content is being used.

I'll give you an example that I've seen all too often. Let's say there is a B2B technology company that is really growing quickly, but where the sales and marketing teams don't communicate very well. Let's assume they are very good at creating thought leadership content. Their white papers are truly educational and helpful. In fact, they are so helpful that a common occurrence is that prospective customers call or email into the sales team and ask follow-up questions. Salespeople routinely field calls where the prospect says, "I just received this amazing white paper from your company. The calculations are extremely helpful. I have a question about them." And the salesperson then says, "I have no idea what you're talking about."

That very short and unfortunate experience does two things. The first is that it immediately ruins the salesperson's relationship with that prospective customer. If it's even possible, they provided *negative* value. They not only can't answer the question, they aren't even aware of why it's being asked. This salesperson is now less than useless to this prospect, because they actually now represent an obstacle to getting an answer they thought they wanted. Secondly, they've now damaged the value of the content itself. The prospect is questioning whether or not the white paper can be trusted. If the very company from where it originated doesn't know how to discuss it, perhaps it's not accurate.

Then, here's the final punch in the gut. If you stack enough of these experiences together, the sales team becomes convinced that this material is not only unhelpful, but actually preventing them from developing relationships with new customers. Word spreads from sales to demand generation teams, and even senior leadership. Requests for content that "has worked before" become standard to the content team. It's a vicious cycle, with no improvement possible.

In this kind of environment, the problems with implementing a new content marketing strategy become vivid indeed. Content marketing practitioners (because they've now suddenly taken on the responsibilities of creating content) are expected to respond to the on-demand needs of the "stakeholders." Yet the content teams themselves rarely count as stakeholders. Every request is valid, and the content team has to act on each. The content team risks becoming an on-demand service designed to produce content like fast food, and there's only one thing on the menu: "More content like what we used to get."

This is not a strategic approach.

Often, we find that business managers will say they have a content strategy when they really don't. They may have identified the people who should be responsible for content, but they haven't put in place a process for how content should be ideated, created, produced, and published. They can point to all the existing content and say, "See, we produce a ton of content." But what they can't do is tell you why or what ideas are being prioritized right now that will become future content, or how it will take shape, or when it will be said. In other words, these businesses only understand what the company has said—but still lack any insight into what it *should* or *is going to* say.

The answer is not just to identify the purpose and charter of the content team, but to build in a governance process for the business that elevates planning, prioritization, collaboration, merchandising, and scheduling of content into the business strategy. Every content marketing strategy needs all of these steps, determining what the teams *will* create, not simply measuring what they have already created.

The opportunity here is to go beyond content marketing to cultivate an organizational awareness of all the marketing content being created, so that the content marketing planning and prioritization happen within the context of all the other content-related activities in other functions.

That sounds like a lot—and it is. But if you're going to ultimately measure a content marketing strategy based on how all your content-related efforts perform together, you must be able to distinguish your priorities for each. Otherwise, it's like trying to understand the durability of your car by only measuring the oil consumption. It's better to understand it in relation to its fuel consumption, number of miles driven, and destinations.

In summary: The new content marketing team's job is not just to be good at content itself, but also to help the rest of the organization to be good at content. It is the only way that any business achieves quality at scale.

Governance enables both quantity and quality

A successful content marketing strategy adds value by improving quality as it facilitates scale. The healthy and visible tension (expressed as a process) between improving quality and facilitating scale means a company will have insight into *how much is enough* and never create too much or too little content. Every business will always create more content. Every new customer, every new product, every new marketplace, every new channel, and every new communication creates a need for more content.

As I said in Chapter 1, content is the operating system for business. If it is a successful operating system that runs smoothly and rarely crashes, then every person—from senior executives to the frontline workers—serves as a coder for that system.

A great content governance process should enable everyone to code at quality. You may prioritize some areas over others in the moment, but the content team's overall mission isn't to pick and choose individual pieces. It's to be aware of the quality of all of it.

The process is more important than the project

One of the challenges of modern technology is that highly produced content is almost too easy to create. Thus, many modern businesses mistake content strategy for the increased speed at which highly produced digital assets can be manufactured upon request.

Instead, successful businesses employ a deliberative process for making choices about *what* ideas should be made into content they should create, in what *order*, and on what *schedule*, in context with all the other requests being made.

However, the idealized notion of "*process*" can lead to another trap businesses fall into. The conventional wisdom is that simply documenting the way things are made or should be made is adequate to create a successful process. In this case, a new team is charged not just with responsibilities, but with documenting the "cookbook" of how things should be prioritized and processed. The new team then tries to convince the rest of the business (the other teams) that this new documented process is the law of the land by sending around the cookbook document for comment or buy-in.

Spoiler alert: That rarely works.

Differentiating a brand through content marketing isn't about having a template for writing the most intelligent white papers, or a rulebook for having the most entertaining podcast, or the style guide for how to make the most compelling blog or video series.

Remember, your content itself provides no long-term competitive advantage. Sustained success comes from having the awareness and active processes to direct all the business's knowledge into the most meaningful activities that provide you the opportunity to create value with content.

So, how do you begin? How do you create the right process that coordinates the responsibilities and the new charter of your content marketing team?

Remember, it's a wicked problem!

Start with questions that have no answers (yet)

Here's a quick story: a large, fast-growing financial services technology company (Fintech it's called) wanted to roll out a new governance model, workflow, and content marketing lifecycle management plan.

As a kickoff to that process, they reviewed best practices and how companies like theirs had solved similar challenges. The people who'd been with the company less than a year rejoiced. They loved it.

On the other hand, the senior leaders and many of the veteran marketing and content practitioners didn't. They agreed that the other companies' solutions sounded fine, but they didn't actually see the problem it would solve in their own organization.

They all simply accepted the responsibilities of various aspects of content creation and management. It was duplicative, inefficient, and extraordinarily hard to understand for anyone who hadn't been at the company for a good amount of time. There were no documented processes, just habits that had been built up over years of "that's the way we do things here."

The tension between the new people's love for the idea of a new process and the veterans' discomfort with it is a great example of management guru Peter Drucker's classic phrase "culture eats strategy for breakfast." You see it all the time in business, where, for example, a new employee comes in for training and the person training them says secretively, "I know the manual says to do it this way, but the real way to get that done is to just call Jim. He's been around forever and knows how to do that thing."

In the case of the Fintech company, senior leadership was so used to seeing (or not seeing, as the case may be) content created and managed in a particular way, they said to their new teams, "We don't see the problem. Content is still getting done. What's the benefit of all this change you're suggesting that seems to be designed to fix something that doesn't appear to be broken?"

The answer, truthfully, was, "We don't know—yet."

Engineer and professor W. Edwards Deming created what he called the System of Profound Knowledge (SoPK). I know it sounds a bit like a *Lord of the Rings* quest, but it's an incredible framework for building systems in business. The idea is that systems/processes cannot understand themselves. For any business process to be measured, improved, or even work, the business (meaning the people in the business) must fully understand the system/process. Without that knowledge, he said, "people will not learn a better way. Their best efforts and hard work only dig deeper the pit that they are working in. Their best efforts and hard work do not provide an outside view of the organization."[1]

But what does all that really mean? For example, I can't say that I really *know* the *process* of writing this book. I don't have a system for it. But I could still predict that I would get it done on time. I seem to know what I'm doing.

But Deming doesn't mean *you* don't know what you're doing. You, alone, might be just fine. He means that the *organization* doesn't know what it's doing. Trust me when I say that if I'd tried to scale the way I wrote this book—or to write more than one—to any team bigger than just me, it would have been a nightmare.

For example, with the Fintech company, two of the veteran global marketing practitioners responsible for producing much of the content marketing for the business were asked to explain to the new teams their process for how the hundreds of content pieces they worked on were selected, planned, and prioritized for distribution.

Here's how they described it step by step:

1 They select articles based on their gut feelings. Sometimes they have email conversations about the options, but sometimes whoever has time chooses what pieces will be created.

2 They list the titles of the chosen content on a spreadsheet, prioritizing each asset by highlighting it in red, yellow, or green. They email a new spreadsheet to each other regularly based on a template they created.

3 They upload the creative briefs to an external file-sharing service because their internal digital asset management software doesn't allow access by the third-party agencies responsible for editing and designing the content marketing articles.

4 The agencies return the fully designed files to the two managers through the external file-sharing service that only they have access to.

5 The global marketing managers determine which, if any, of the articles should go out to the regional offices and email those files to the local marketing managers in the correct offices.

How were other regional offices made aware of the content? How were the produced article assets made centrally available? What if someone needed the original "raw" content and not the final designed assets? Well, the managers had answers to those questions. "*We* email the offices when *we* have time and remember to do it. *We* upload some of the assets to a shared internal server once a month. And if somebody needs raw content *we* can always go back and ask the agency for it."

Then, they were asked the question that really had no answer. What if "*we*" goes away? In other words, what if those two managers won the lottery and left the business unexpectedly? Whose responsibility is it to unwind the ball of tangled asset-creation twine for some new person, or even make it run like it used to?

They shrugged and laughed, and said they weren't thinking about the lottery.

Clean the occurrent kitchen

Let's return to the question that the senior-level executives asked. How can you answer similar questions about the potential value of fixing problems the business doesn't know exist?

Just like the two global regional marketing managers, you can't. You may know what the result was in other organizations, but you can't know exactly what will happen in your situation. It kind of works as is. And it's also kind of broken. You just don't know.

But what you can do is to develop a culture of examining occurrent behavior.

Occurrent behavior is what *really* happens in the business vs. what is supposed to happen or what the business perceives is happening.

The Fintech company story offers a great example. From the senior leadership's perspective, nothing was broken. They perceived the operating process of those two global marketing managers as working. When shown the documented "process" (very loosely defined) of how it was actually happening, they said, "That's not the way it was designed to work. But if it's working, it's working."

That acknowledgment is an example of what's called "tacit knowledge." It's the "everybody just kinda knows" process. Whenever anyone responds to a question with "that's the way it's always been done," you can be pretty sure tacit knowledge is at play. These are simply habits that develop in business over time and eventually become the "culture." Stack enough of them together and you have a corporate culture that will eat strategy for breakfast every time.

Does that mean that it's "unfixable"? Not at all. You just have to be willing to implement a new process that doesn't necessarily promise to fix something the business believes is broken. In other words, create a *new* process that promises to be new, and nothing else.

Examine your content culture and strategy

Ironically, the first step in fixing a bad process is to audit and document it. This is one of the best ways to identify where communication and collaboration are being assumed in the transformation of ideas into actual useful content.

You're going to do two examinations. The first is to conduct an audit, a review, or a simple set of experiments, to thoroughly examine the occurrent behavior of your content strategy. What's really going on.

Then, you're going to do that same exercise again—but you're going to design how it *should* happen.

Here's how to do this process:

1 Audit: Figure out what's really going on
Develop a team (maybe it's just you) to examine and document the occurrent behavior around your content. How does it move from ideation to creation, management, activation, publishing, measuring, and archiving? If necessary, start with one area, such as thought leadership content, or just the blog, or even just sales materials. Or even better, start cross-functionally, but focus on just one area of the customer's journey (maybe "Awareness Content"). Document what actually happens (not what's supposed to happen). Identify and categorize the obvious challenges and where approaches go outside perceived models (even for good reason).

2 Design: Work through how the process would ideally work
Now, work through with your team (again, maybe it's just you) how it should actually work. You don't have to get to every detail, but simply look at what makes the most sense and could be a repeatable way to do things so that the *organization* knows what it's doing and can explain it.

3 Plot: Note the obvious gaps and inevitable costs
With the gaps documented, identify (if you can) the extraneous costs, missed opportunities, or high-probability risks if the current habits remain. For example, at the Fintech company, the siloed content creation process with the two managers prompted employees to create new, duplicative content rather than reuse content created from another silo. They found one singular topic had 32 versions redone as ebooks, articles, blog posts, and infographics. What is the cost of the time spent on 31 unnecessary content assets?

4 Observe: Take a dragonfly view of estimating the challenge
Dragonflies see 360 degrees around themselves. People don't. No one can develop a perspective that encompasses every aspect of every business process. But after looking at one area, you may be able to estimate the value of fixing these habits across multiple functional areas, or for more than one area of responsibility. Look at the costs for the obvious things (like the 31 extra content assets). Assume similar issues lie in other unexamined areas and extrapolate the costs. Include estimates based on what organizations similar to yours have found, if you can.

These steps should give you a helpful estimate of the value of developing or improving all of your strategic content processes.

Remember that people (and businesses) are reluctant to change, especially when they're not feeling pain. But take heart and ask to prototype these examples as net new processes. After working on more than 300 content marketing strategy engagements, I've found that companies that struggle to build a case for changing existing processes are most often the ones that succeed by simply creating new ones from scratch. These new processes become the new, better way of doing things, and ultimately replace the old.

Perspective as a process

One way to build a mechanism to try new processes and get continual perspective into what's working is this: Once you have the purposes and processes identified and accounted for, form a cross-functional team to encourage collaboration, and to help the business adhere to a new process.

You might call it an accountability board, or an editorial board—or even a content committee. Whatever your name for it, I like to compare it to creating an "air traffic control" tower for your content strategy. This group may not control all the planes in the sky, but once it has visibility and alignment into everything that's up there, it has incentive to manage it in an orderly fashion.

While the executive leadership team sets the content team's responsibilities and establishes budgets and governance models, the editorial board is a cross-functional group assembled from the company's major stakeholders and subject matter experts. The content marketing strategy leader facilitates the board.

This group focuses on the content marketing strategy, helping to create an aligned approach, deciding on a few (or fewer) proactive big ideas, and moving these ideas to a development process. The bigger stories can be repurposed into smaller assets for other parts of the organization that need them.

Now, again, it might sound like I'm proposing an over-engineered bureaucracy for content marketing. I'm not. Once you understand all the occurrent behavior, you can certainly make a business decision on how much the editorial board will guide. The whole point is to get a group together—even if it's just you and your boss—to say this is the content that's being demanded, and this is the content we want to plan, and this is what all of that implies about what we want to say as a business. Let's all agree on which of these ideas, requests, and needs we want to manage.

Doing this addresses one of the biggest hurdles for a successful content marketing strategy—striking a balance between the overarching goals and the demands to act as an internal content support organization for the rest of the business (i.e., an on-demand content factory) and creating a shared understanding of what the brand *should* or *will* say in the future.

The illustration here shows how the content marketing team is supported by nine typical roles and responsibilities to execute the projects determined to be priorities by the editorial board. You can see that a content marketing leader (perhaps that's you) facilitates the communication between the company's leadership and the editorial board.

Remember, our purpose decided the broad categories of responsibilities that the content marketing team would take on. Now we are basing the roles of the content team, and a governing body, to help us set the right process for those responsibilities.

Content projects then become the responsibility of the content creation execution team, including individuals from any part of the organization, freelancers, or creative agencies.

Figure 4.2 The Editorial Board and Content Team

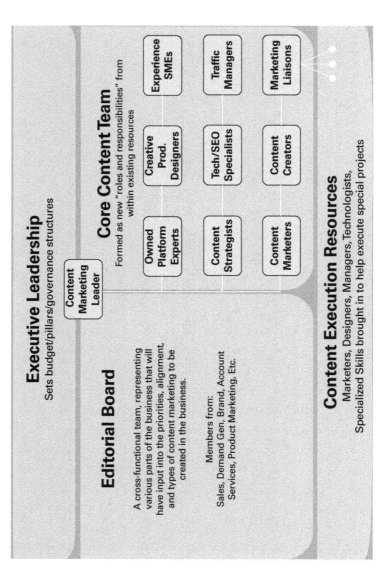

Executive Leadership
Sets budget/pillars/governance structures

Content Marketing Leader

Editorial Board

A cross-functional team, representing various parts of the business that will have input into the priorities, alignment, and types of content marketing to be created in the business.

Members from:

Sales, Demand Gen, Brand, Account Services, Product Marketing, Etc.

Core Content Team
Formed as new "roles and responsibilities" from within existing resources

Owned Platform Experts

Creative Prod. Designers

Experience SMEs

Content Strategists

Tech/SEO Specialists

Traffic Managers

Content Marketers

Content Creators

Marketing Liaisons

Content Execution Resources
Marketers, Designers, Managers, Technologists, Specialized Skills brought in to help execute special projects

NOTE This illustrates how a content marketing team may be constructed from different roles and responsibilities, with a content marketing leader acting as the liaison between an editorial board and executive leadership. In smaller companies, these may be one and the same.

Would you like to see the "role descriptions" for each of the nine roles on the content team? We have it available exclusively for readers of this book at ContentMarketingStrategy.com

Responsibilities of the editorial board

The editorial board should meet regularly. Depending on the scale of content marketing in the business, it can be responsible for these outputs:

- Setting creative priorities, points of view, and thought leadership vision
- Reviewing measurement of content marketing efforts and deciding on topics or channels based on that analysis
- Prioritizing and/or setting urgency for the content marketing calendar
- Guiding and/or setting editorial guidelines, tone, or standards
- Suggesting topics or unique needs for departmental/functional strategies
- Helping set promotional strategies for larger content initiatives
- Guiding resourcing/budgeting priorities

The board's output is a shared editorial production and publishing calendar that balances ad hoc asset needs from different departments and a proactive and strategic approach to larger content projects.

For example, I know of one content team that struggled to keep their thought leadership blog current and compelling because they had other demands from the product and sales enablement teams who wanted more and more customer success stories and technical how-to articles. The content team had no time or resources to tackle the stated strategy of creating content that evangelized their disruptive approach in the industry.

To address that problem, the company decided to create a more proactive content approach and facilitate it through an editorial board. The content marketing team helped to assemble a cross-functional group made up of marketing, demand generation, enterprise sales, account services, and brand. The board meets twice a month to set the direction and priority of content marketing in the business.

Additionally, the content team assembled external subject matter experts who met every other month with the editorial board to suggest new topics and angles for their thought leadership.

Now, because the content marketing team's charter was right about in the middle between the Producer and Product models, the company decided on a 60–40 percent balance for content creation resources: Proactive content projects that were focused for their blog but that could be repurposed across the business (60 percent) vs. unique on-demand assets created for individual departments (40 percent). New ideas and requests that come to the content team are collected until the editorial board meets.

See how all this starts to work together?

Figure 4.3 shows how the content decision and creation process works.

1 **Ideation:** There is some form of an intake process. Again, this may be limited to only one type of content, or one area that you are trying to optimize in marketing. But whether that's a dedicated email, a Slack channel, or a form that is filled out, all requests for content of this type go through this mechanism.

2 **Planning:** The editorial board—in collaboration with the content team—prioritizes the new projects and determines which needs can be fulfilled by smaller executions within larger projects (e.g., a customer success story, testimonial, podcast interview, webinar with a customer). The results of this step are a shared calendar, clear resource allocation, aligned goals and objectives, and a project list and bill of materials (a to-do list if you will) of content to be created.

3 **Creation:** These content/editorial projects are executed. But this is where content is planned and researched, then written, edited, and ultimately structured in some way with an eye toward multiple uses and the different assets that will ultimately be designed.

4 **Production:** This is where ideas become experiences. The content and creative briefs are turned over to the designers who will plan for the experiences that will express these ideas. They will design the containers, be they images, videos, text, or combinations of those things, that will result in the finished assets.

Figure 4.3 The Editorial Process

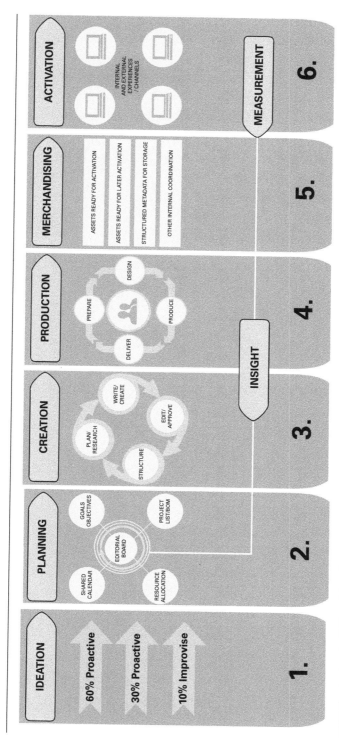

NOTE The structured activities of the editorial process should align with a well-formed and repeatable process with at least six major steps.

5 Merchandising: Once they are created, these assets need to be made ready for activation. They will have metadata associated with them and will be moved to digital asset repositories or file folders. Other teams will be notified they are finished. This step is the internal coordination of all these digital assets, including those that may not be needed or utilized for some time.

6 Activation: This is the publishing and promotion of these digital assets out to the channels and/or platforms on which they will be consumed by audiences. It also includes the kickoff of any promotional activities that will be done to promote this new content to intended audiences.

From there, there will be a measurement step (that we will discuss in detail in Chapter 8), and then the insight gleaned from the goals and objectives set in Step 2 will be aligned with this insight in order to optimize the process going forward.

With this process, content planning and creation are more strategic. Here are some of the benefits:

- **Better scalability:** Core editorial topics and ideas are discussed and proposed among teams and brought together in the central editorial board. The cross-functional editorial board synthesizes, packages, and prioritizes content bills of materials (BOM) of assets to be created.

- **More efficient production:** Assets move through a production process—and versions created—even if they will not be used for some time. Thus, assets are leveraged more effectively to address multiple purposes.

- **Better findability:** The content team doesn't handle all content creation but does handle all content flow. Assets are managed and published by trained managers (experts) into the CMS and DAM, accounting for metadata, structures, and reuse.

By adopting this editorial board approach, which was done in phases, the company transformed its content marketing by scaling a few big content ideas into many iterations and executions at different parts of the journey.

Start small, scale big

Part of this team's success is attributed to starting small. The content marketing leader had a team of three. Before having executive support, she started with the demand generation group and implemented an informal sharing meeting. The content team would share their to-do list, then align it with what the demand generation team needed, and both teams would agree on priorities. Slowly, representatives from other teams joined the meeting to form the fully realized editorial board. They shifted to more proactive projects instead of the on-demand requests.

Many times, full-scale change management can sound daunting. But mark my words, if your content marketing program is ever going to scale to address multiple parts of the customer experience or to serve more than a tiny fraction of the marketing strategy, governance must be core to your approach.

Governance is the ability to manage a creative process

Ultimately, you don't have to think of "governance" as bureaucracy, institutionalized cookbooks, or even defined powers. When it comes to your content marketing strategy, think of it as answering a relatively simple question: How will we all consistently decide what ideas should become content and when, how, and where should we create, manage, activate, promote, and measure it?

An assembly of an editorial board can be a great step in answering that question, with new processes that may solve unobvious challenges, but, more importantly, create new opportunities.

People aren't wrong to be reluctant to change how they work. If they can't understand the problem, looking at solutions can be confusing. A common pushback I hear when recommending these kinds of changes to content responsibilities and governance processes is "We don't know how." This response usually doesn't come from the practitioners but from senior leadership. Their reluctance to adopt a fundamentally new process happens because the organization doesn't

understand it. It is unfortunate that "not knowing how" then trans-
lates to the equivalent of "we can't do it"—all because the perception
is that the effort of learning something new outweighs losing the mo-
mentum of "doing it the way we've always done it." It's like when
your dad always takes the long way to drive to the beach because
"Dammit, that's the way I know!"

Ultimately, you need to be comfortable with only one change—
increasing the capacity to change. Businesses add more and more
interfaces, content types, and complex workflows every day. Sales,
marketing, product design, customer service, the agency, and your
partners all engage directly with your audiences.

As you begin to exercise this new business muscle of content marketing, customer experience, and expanded customer touchpoints,
you should understand that all these goals depend on your ability to
create new. New what? New everything. You just have to try new.

Independent of where you sit in the organization, you have the power
to develop these new maps. It's a choice—you can continue to only fix
things in such disrepair as to qualify for demolition, or you can look at
things that might be better (or not) and try a new way of doing it.

Your new way might work or it might not. But at least you'll have
a new perspective. And a new perspective almost always brings new
opportunities.

Okay, now it's time for us to pivot away from all this process stuff,
and the coordination of content, and operations, and start focusing
on the reason we're doing all this work to begin with: the audience.

We have included the role descriptions, a template for mapping designed
content processes, and a framework for mapping the occurrent behavior
in your company. Use this and the follow-on workbook to map out your
processes, and connect them to the responsibilities of your team. It's
available at ContentMarketingStrategy.com

Note

1 Edwards Deming, W. (2018) *The New Economics for Industry,
Government, Education*, Cambridge, MA: MIT Press, p.68

Understanding Audiences 05

Engaging and Subscribing Audiences Is the Heart of Content Marketing

An audience may just be the modern business's most valuable asset.

Here is one of the most important reasons that content marketing is perhaps the most integral part of any modern marketing strategy. You ready?

All audiences are customers, but only some customers buy our products.

Let me explain.

As we can hopefully agree by this point, content marketing is not a replacement for traditional marketing. But the activities are different enough from a classic marketing approach to require a different way of operation.

If we are ever to truly succeed with a content marketing strategy, we must provide for the capability to drive multiple lines of value for our business. This means that we must look beyond a simple "sales" transaction or revenue as the only means of driving business value.

Peter Drucker once said that the purpose of business is to "create a customer." This is true. But many marketers (and other business executives) take the term "customer" too literally.

Many think a customer is created when a person purchases a company's product or solution. I argue that a one-time sales transaction does *not* necessarily mean you've created a true customer (certainly not in the spirit of the Drucker definition). Similarly, businesses can create valuable customers who haven't purchased any product or service.

As Drucker himself said, "It is the customer who determines what a business is. For it is the customer who, through being willing to pay for a good or for a service, converts economic resources into wealth, things into goods."[1] Great marketing provides value that customers are willing to invest in, and that creates wealth for the business. But not all customer investments must involve a purchase. As media companies have long realized, customers can also provide value like time, attention, referrals, personal data, and brand loyalty, all of which can be converted in varying degrees into wealth for the business.

One television executive stated two decades ago in the book *Audience Economics*: "I can't think of another business that makes one product but sells a different product. We make programs and put them on the air. We are not selling the programs; we are selling the people that watch the programs."[2] Translated to a 2023 media business model: We create content, and we sell access to the people who consume that content.

This business model has become one of the most popular means of driving economic value in today's digital media-driven world. As of the writing of this book, of the top six companies with a market capitalization of more than $1 trillion, four of them either wholly or partially utilize the business model of "we create content, and we sell access to the people who consume that content": Apple, Microsoft, Alphabet, and Amazon. And each one of those companies also sells other products and services to their customers.

As I said at the beginning of this book, none of those companies would recognize (or maybe acknowledge is the better word) that "content marketing" is what they are doing. But it is.

Why shouldn't we mere mortal companies avail ourselves of the same business model?

Content marketing offers traditional product and service companies an opportunity to expand the classic definition of a customer and expand how wealth can be created in the business.

"But wait a minute," you might say. "How? We aren't media companies."

What is the evolution of marketing's value?

Remember from Chapter 1, modern marketers are measured by their ability to *efficiently* move prospective buyers through a process. Theoretically, every step a buyer takes in that process increases their value to the business. Realistically (because of the focus on efficiency), the only step that traditionally matters is the "purchase" step, as that's how most businesses define creating a customer (someone buys their product or service).

However, today, most marketing departments value a qualified lead higher than a generic visitor. A sales opportunity (or a filled shopping cart), says the marketer, is worth more to the business than a qualified lead, and a sale is worth more than a filled shopping cart. But, much to the marketer's chagrin, the business turns its head on that value. It values the entirety of the marketing effort by simply dividing the total marketing dollars spent by the sum of the revenue created at each of those stage gates.

In other words, most marketers value marketing based on its ability to efficiently attract more, and more interested, people at each of those stage gates. But most businesses ultimately measure marketing based on its ability to create sales transactions.

A typical marketing return on investment (ROI) calculation for a business might look something like this:

$$(((A \times B \times C) - D) \div D) \times 100 = ROI\%$$

I know you may have been told there is no math in content marketing, but this equation isn't nearly as complicated as it looks. Here is a description of the variables:

A Is the number of leads generated. Different companies might define this number using different stage gates. One might base it on visitors, and another might look only at visitors who are qualified or show interest in purchasing. Any of these will do, because the more important number is the next one.

B Is the lead-to-customer rate. How many of those leads ultimately became a customer? Unless you're some kind of wizard, this number is a lot less than one—and usually expressed as a percentage (e.g., 1%, 2%).

C Is the average initial transaction (sales) price paid by an average customer.

D Is the total cost of your marketing. Again, different companies calculate this in a variety of ways. It may just be your advertising spend, or it may also include every marketing cost including the wages of people who put time into this marketing effort.

It doesn't take a mathematician to see some of the challenges with this calculation from the marketer's perspective. In the simplest sense, this calculation only credits marketing investment with generating the most leads, with the lowest cost, at the highest average transaction. Now, the marketer does usually have influence over three of those variables (usually A, B, and D). So my strategy as a marketing manager becomes optimizing whichever of the three I can. We ask questions:

- Can I simply use my budget to generate more and more leads to meet my ROI?
- Can I increase my budget to get more (or better) leads to meet my ROI?
- Can I make my content more compelling to convert more of the leads I'm getting to meet my ROI?

If we simply break this calculation down to its base level, it is spend/revenue. How much did you spend in exchange for how much revenue? Is it any wonder then that many marketers feel like their budgets are unfairly aligned with revenue numbers?

However, some marketers will often measure the "*potential* revenue" as part of their calculations. This is especially true where there is a separate sales process that is distinct from marketing. Marketing will claim to have created X number of leads that can potentially equate to Y amount of revenue. Then, it becomes the sales team's job to meet that standard.

But this approach is challenged as well.

Many marketers will claim, rightfully, that engaged, interested people at any of those stage gates (lead, qualified lead, opportunity, etc.) are also valuable to the company. It is just unrealized—or potential—future revenue. But how much value does an unrealized visitor, lead, or qualified opportunity really have? The CFO's answer is "zero" since those potential customers never purchased anything, and the revenue-to-marketing-cost ratio is the only thing that matters. But marketers are also correct. It's also *not* zero, because the activity did generate something worth more than a generic visitor. Right? Maybe they don't buy this month, but maybe they'll come back? Maybe they lost budget, but they will recommend us to a friend? Maybe they buy something else? Maybe.

So, any marketer claiming to have created financial value by generating more "engaged visitors" or more "targeted leads" often gets the side-eye from the CFO, who's thinking (à la Jerry Maguire), "Show me the money."

How does content marketing offer a way to solve this conundrum and expand the classic definition of a customer and how wealth can be created in the business?

What if businesses looked at some or all of those unrealized visitors, leads, and qualified sales as a media company would?

What if the business saw a relationship with audiences as marketers see their relationship with customers? What if the business viewed the ability to reach them as an asset that can increase in value over time?

In such a business, you wouldn't simply measure the size of the audience. You would measure how much the audience—specifically the different kinds of audience members—adds wealth to the business. In other words, you would operate like a media company: You would create content and create business value by establishing a relationship to the people who consume that content and by leveraging the value they provide to the business.

Measuring the value of relationships with customers tells us so much more about the health of the business than simply measuring the number of paid transactions. This is something that today's media companies understand. The astronomical business value of media companies like Meta, Google, Netflix, Amazon (yes, it is partially a media company), and others isn't based only on the fact that they can reach millions (or billions) of people. Their business value comes because they reach millions of people who actively, willingly, and trustingly desire to be reached by them.

For example, Amazon Prime Video is estimated to have 70 million users and to generate about $2.5 billion in revenue for the company (at the time of writing). Consider that, in 2022, Amazon spent approximately $15 billion on video content for Amazon Prime. No matter how many marketing ROI calculations you do, those numbers won't work as a standalone business. And that's because they don't have to. Amazon Prime Video is a content marketing strategy that enables Amazon to reach and engage more people willing to spend more money to subscribe to Amazon's suite of products and services. When you understand that Prime members spend double (yes, double) what non-Prime members spend annually, you can start to see why Amazon sees Prime Video audiences as a key component of their marketing strategy.

But, okay, that is Amazon. How does your ever so much slightly smaller business assign a monetary value to someone in your audience who actively and willingly participates with your brand but may not now (or ever) spend money on your product or service? The answer to that question is, however, "Just like Amazon did." We must redefine how we see "customer."

Audience valuation: Redefining customers

Let's back up a minute.

Have you heard this classic joke? An economist, a physicist, and a chemist are stranded on a desert island. One day a can of food washes up on the beach. The physicist and chemist each devise ingenious methods to open the can. The physicist tries to fashion a tool out of rocks to cut the can. The chemist discusses how to create an acid out of seawater to dissolve the can. When it is the economist's turn he simply says, "OK, assume there is a can opener."

Here's what the joke is really about: What economists do in terms of predicting company or market performance is a fuzzy science that relies on assumptions.

In a similar way, valuing audiences is fuzzy and complex even for media companies where this is common practice. Assigning a real monetary value to the audience's investment of time, data, attention, loyalty, and engagement hinges a lot on what we actually *do* with that participation. Remember, for Amazon it's not just that they have the Prime Video audience, it's what they *do* with that audience (leverage that relationship with them to market other products and services) that encourages them to spend double the amount.

Exploring how to establish audience valuation is not as much an accounting exercise as it is a marketing exercise that helps you apply monetary value to other parts of the business. In other words, to paraphrase the media company executive quoted earlier, you're not valuing the content the audience consumes, you're valuing the *audiences* that consume the content. Ask yourself, by developing a better, deeper relationship with them will they:

- Do more on our behalf? Share more? Spread the word about us?
- Behave in a way we like with greater frequency?
- Tell us things that provide insight and help us grow better, faster, more efficiently? Act as a multiplier to our other efforts?

Our first step is to define our audience, and the simplest definition of "audience" (from the dictionary) is a group of people who gather to view or listen to performances or who consume or admire content—a book, art, or other media. For your purposes as a content marketer, audiences are groups of people willing to invest their time, attention, and actions on the content you create.

Now, remember the "reach and frequency" mantra from marketing strategy. If your goal is to put a tangible financial value on the depth and dimension of the investment the audience makes (e.g., the relationship), then it makes sense to place a higher value on audience members you can reach whenever you desire. In other words, place higher value on audience members who not only give you permission to reach them as frequently as you'd like, but also give you this information willingly and consistently. Let's call them "subscribers."

This is what makes subscribers measurable. They are addressable. A subscriber is someone you know you can reach (and confirm you've reached) any time you choose. That immediately separates them from audiences on third-party platforms such as Facebook ("likes") or Twitter ("followers") or podcasts (listeners), where an algorithm (or a walled garden) from that third-party platform interferes (or plays middleman) with your ability to identify who has been reached, and when.

So, let's refine the definition of an audience asset to say that the goal is to measure *addressable subscribers to your content*.

> *One author's note here: I realize that, even as I write this book, new technologies are emerging that may enable different platforms to be addressable even without a subscriber providing an email, phone number, physical address, or other elements of personal data. So, while these "addresses" are what define a subscriber today, technology may help us redefine that in the coming years.*

In defining an audience asset, you can limit it to people who have provided identifiable information that allows you to deliver messages to them at your choosing.

With that in mind, how do you research and identify the most valuable audiences? You build audience personas.

Audience personas: Moving beyond buyer personas

Wait—what's a buyer persona, and why are we moving beyond them?

Buyer personas have been an important part of marketing strategy for the last few decades. They are defined as research-based archetypal (modeled) representations of who buyers are, what they are trying to accomplish, what goals drive their behavior, how they think, how they buy, and how they decide what to buy and when.

This is a perfect definition of a person you want to understand after they self-identify as someone who has a specific need for your product or service.

For the record, I'm a huge proponent of buyer persona development. I think it is a critical part of helping product- and service-focused marketers and sales teams understand how to bring their product into the marketplace. It's a critical element of the "product" component of the 4 Ps.

Buyer personas help you understand how to position features and benefits and value propositions in describing and distributing your product and the marketing for it. Buyer personas help you define the best place for distribution of or access to your product. Buyer personas help differentiate pricing strategies you may need to employ. And buyer personas help you determine the right promotional mix for your integrated plan. In the simplest terms, buyer personas put your company/product/service at the center of the story and your task becomes creating the strongest pull of gravity to attract more people to that center.

However, as you develop buyer personas, what if you started with the customer's need at the center of the story? In other words, what if, rather than starting with an answer (the product), and then attempting to figure out what attributes or fulfillment might lead the audience there—you started with the question, "What do you (potential buyer) need/want?" What if you started with the audience's interests, challenges, and questions—well before and/or after they have a need for your particular solution—and then figured out what your unique answer might be.

That gives you an audience persona. And, as it turns out, if we reach back into our product marketing toolkit, we can find a perfect approach to this much broader question.

Audience personas and the jobs to be done

If you're not familiar with the jobs-to-be-done theory, it's an extraordinarily powerful framework to get to new, innovative product ideas.

To be clear, this theory is neither new nor my invention. The history of the approach can be linked to the late 1960s when marketing professors Chester Wasson and David McConaughy suggested customers don't buy products, but rather what they then called a "satisfaction bundle" for solving problems.

And one of my marketing heroes, Harvard professor Theodore Levitt, suggested back in the 1960s that products themselves had no intrinsic value—that customers use products and services to solve problems. This was the birth of his now-famous quote: "*People don't want to buy a quarter-inch drill, they want a quarter-inch hole.*" In other words, people don't buy a product because of the product, they buy it because it will provide progress toward a job that they want or need completed.

The jobs-to-be-done theory really gained traction through an idea called outcome-driven innovation in the late 1990s, and it was popularized in Clayton Christensen's 2003 book *The Innovator's Solution*.

The jobs-to-be-done theory is rich, and quite a powerful way to develop new ideas and positioning for innovation in a marketplace.

In the world of developing audience personas, I have a small twist on the jobs-to-be-done theory and have found it to be an extraordinarily helpful tool for getting to a much more useful audience persona profile for a content marketing strategy. It opens a wider set of opportunities for a brand's stories. It helps broaden the story to theoretically cover the audience's entire journey, and it can also be extraordinarily specific, helping the brand get to what my colleague and CMI founder Joe Pulizzi calls the "content tilt"—a worldview that your brand is the best at delivering.

We've used this approach for years in our workshops and advisory engagements, customizing it a bit for audience development. It breaks down into five steps that we call the Five Ds of Audience Persona Development:

1 Define your target: Detail the total addressable audience.

2 Discover the "so I can": Uncover all (or many) of the jobs to be done.

3 Decide on your niche: Find your sweet spot among what you've discovered.

4 Differentiate your content approach: Detail where your sweet spot meets your goals and objectives.

5 Design the success statements: Break down the jobs into meaningful categories to help direct the value you can provide.

Let's look at each of these.

Step 1: Define your target audience and its size

When defining a target audience, it's critical to go beyond the traditional segmentation of demographics such as age, geography, income levels, and job titles. Make sure to open the question to a wide variety of interests and/or challenges because you're not using interest in your product or service as the common foundation.

Of course, you're typically not starting with a blank slate here, either. It would be overwhelming and unhelpful to simply say, "Let's look at anything our target audience might be interested in or challenged with." At least focus on the general topic area of your business.

As we'll see in Step 3, the more niche you can be with a targeted audience, the better your chance of finding a differentiated approach. However, you also want to balance this by quantifying the target audience to ensure that it is ultimately a viable number (big enough) to justify pursuing.

Just as every single marketer should know the size of their total addressable market (TAM), every content marketer should know the size of their total addressable audience in or outside of that TAM.

For example, let's say a company wants to target small, entrepreneurial law firms with thought leadership content that would lead them to conclude that they needed the types of research software and services the company provides.

The company's research reveals there are approximately 50,000 US law firms with two or more people. Further, 90 percent of those firms have more than one person but fewer than 10 people. So, the TAM for its products and services would be 45,000 (each business will buy the software only once). But remember, audiences aren't just buyers. Audience size is different.

The average number of partners in these firms is three. Any one of these partners may be the source of a referral, start their own firm, or simply influence whoever makes these kinds of decisions. So, from an *audience* perspective, the total addressable *audience* is 135,000, or three times the TAM.

How do content marketers get this information? The same way that any industrious media company would get it. A few examples:

- Media companies often provide kits to advertisers detailing the population, research, and targeted nature of their target audience. These can offer great insight.

- Professional associations often provide detailed research on the members of their profession, the state of the industry, and the detailed psychographics of these members.

- National, state, and local governments provide free statistics and research on different types of targeted audiences.

- Analyst firms often provide paid access to research products that can provide estimates of total addressable markets in specific marketplaces.

Remember, this is a process—an activity—not a simple project. Do not spend all your time on Step 1. Your estimates will get better over time. For now, get the best estimates and definition you can, and move on to Step 2.

Step 2: Discover the "so i can" by uncovering the jobs to be done

In defining an audience, a job to be done is not just an audience "need." For example, the statement "I need directions" doesn't compel me to use a particular map or mapping resource. However, the statement "I need directions because I'm bringing my family on a trip and we all hate reading maps" is both social and contextual. It helps to define a very specific functional and emotional job to be done.

As you research your target audiences, take the time to go talk with them. Visit with them and research them. This is not a typical focus group, where marketers bring in random customers and listen for their opinions on the brand's product. This is truly meeting with audiences to understand their needs and wants generally and—most importantly—to listen for those social and contextual enhancements to their needs.

One pattern to listen for is this:

When I am _____ I need _____ so I can _____.

For example, in a discussion, a potential audience member for that tech company targeting small law firms might say:

When I'm working, I don't need more software, I need automated research tools that give me freedom so I can have peace of mind and spend more time on my business.

The "so I can" in that sentence is the big clue about the job to be done. If we focus only on the need, we might conclude that the audience member wants a list of research tools that provide automated ways to work more efficiently. In fact, the real job to be done is to provide value that gives that audience member more peace of mind and allows them to spend more time working on their business. In a way, it's almost exactly the opposite of just providing a list of tools.

The point of our content (or our big story) is not to provide more information on tools (that's like Levitt's quarter-inch drill). Rather, our focus should be on how to deliver interesting things that help entrepreneurs achieve "peace of mind and spend more time on their business" (the quarter-inch hole in the wall).

Now, of course, not every person will express everything the same way. But we can look for the patterns and group them together.

Would you like to see a sample questionnaire that you can use to brainstorm a conversation with your audiences, and that can generate these kinds of answers? It's available at ContentMarketingStrategy.com

That gets us to Step 3.

Step 3: Decide on your niche—find the sweet spot

Once you've assembled the size of the audiences and started to catalog the jobs to be done, you can begin to explore and make decisions about which ones you want to solve. You can look at two levers in this next level of brainstorming: size of the job vs. size of the audience.

First, look at how underserved these jobs are. How many others in your marketplace of ideas are trying to solve them? Think of it like this: As you work on your audience personas, you may decide it's better to solve a small, niche job for a huge audience. Or you may decide to solve a huge job for a niche audience.

For example, let's say your business is in retail banking. Would you rather try to solve some specific niche part of financial education for millennials? Or would you rather identify a new niche audience (maybe young parents who are branching into home-based businesses) and solve the entirety of their financial education? Neither answer is wrong—but the conscious choice is critical. Give yourself that flexibility.

The decision is a great example of what Joe Pulizzi calls "the sweet spot." As he says, it's "the intersection between your customer's pain points and where you have the most authority with your stories."[3]

Of course, the choice here should be made in the context of your overall marketing objective and the charter you have chosen as your initial content marketing strategy.

Step 4: Differentiate—go beyond the sweet spot

In the simplest sense, our sweet spot is the relevance we seek to provide for an audience. It is where "what we want to say" meets "what they want to hear."

But to put it bluntly, today relevance is simply table stakes. Anybody can be relevant. To make a difference, you must find differentiation in the sweet spots.

Once you've identified the underserved audiences, cataloged all the jobs you could do, and discovered the relevant sweet spots, you must then prioritize the jobs to be done by those that you should/could solve uniquely because of your distinct point of view on how to solve it.

In other words, if your brand doesn't have differentiated expertise, has no particular point of view, or (by some corporate mandate) cannot develop a new, differentiated point of view on solving that job— then perhaps that job is not yours to solve.

Again, there are two levers here that you might pull and push. Thinking like a media operation, you can decide how you want to differentiate. You could, for example, choose a relatively common (or popular) point of view but solve it through a unique context. Or you could choose a common context and choose to provide a unique point of view.

For example, consider ServiceNow. They are a mid-sized software company focused on providing technology platforms to enhance workflow and project management across larger enterprises.

The company's editorial site, *Workflow*, launched in 2018. The team associated with that was squarely in the Product purpose category and looked at the publication as one of the core products of the company. Its goal was to engage C-level audiences with thought leadership about workflow and how it demonstrably helped create better financial results.

Sexy, right?

ServiceNow's editor-in-chief and director, Richard McGill Murphy, said that the goal of the publication was to cover "technology in the service of people rather than the other way around."[4]

But anyone who has ever looked at targeting C-level executives knows that this is far too broad a way to describe an audience. CFOs are different than CEOs, who are different than CMOs. But ServiceNow aligned around a very niche topic for a broad audience and presented it through a common context: a web publication.

Then, they took the time to start to segment and learn which elements of C-level audiences were engaging the most. As their nomination form for the content marketing award that they ultimately won explains, "We combined engaged time and article metadata, then made narrow audiences on LinkedIn where we could gain certainty about (the reader's) title."

For example, they realized that audience members with titles such as "chief human resource officer" have very different desires than people who have a "vice president of HR" title at similar companies. They also learned that these human resources executives were the most engaged readers.

That insight, plus the incredible number of sales opportunities that ServiceNow receives from the publication, makes it simply one of the most valuable marketing efforts they can do.

That gets us to the last step...

Step 5: Design the map of success—document the audience journey

Once you have identified the ideal jobs and the ideal audience, you can map the high-level success statements for each step the audience takes to solve that job. Is this journey mapping? Yes, but again, it's not a customer journey or a buyer's journey—it's the audience journey for the steps they take to get that job done (or not done, as the case may be).

The goal is to identify the kinds of value (as many as you can) that you can provide across steps of this job to be done. One structure you might consider for each success statement is:

value action | metric | job action | contextual/social clarification

For example, going back to our small business law partner audience, a success statement might be:

Figure 5.1   The Success Statement Diagram

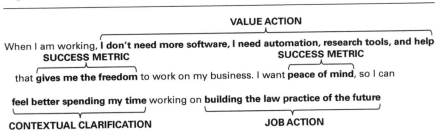

NOTE One can break apart success statements into component parts that begin to provide both a set of messaging key words and phrases and focus for your content.

Once you've categorized these success statements, you might then roll them up into one larger success statement that exemplifies exactly the overall success of that persona.

Ultimately, after all the research, interviews, brainstorming, and clarifying, we can take these steps and assemble our audience persona profile. This will be become an archetype of the jobs-to-be-done that we use to guide our content creation.

A great content marketing strategy places the focus on the continual growth of the audience as an asset with many, many attributes.

These are people who trust you, engage with you, want to hear from you, and will—over time—exchange value with your business in many ways.

In addition to the sample questionnaire, we have provided the complete process for audience persona development in an ebook available exclusively for readers of this book. It's available at ContentMarketingStrategy.com

Investment goals for the audience asset?

Ultimately, there are only two ways to add value to a business: saving costs or increasing revenue. As your audience grows and the purpose of your charter is coming to fruition, you can start to assemble specific business goals that accomplish one or more of those objectives.

Here are a few hypothesized goals to consider:

- Use the first-party data from audiences to increase efficiency of your traditional media buy or consumer research, or to drive better personalization in an e-commerce channel. ServiceNow utilizes first-party audience data to get insights into the most popular C-level titles and to create specifically targeted and personalized advertising to potential customers.

- Sell access to your audience's high traffic and content engagement to non-competitive companies. Cleveland Clinic's blog features advertising from non-competitive companies and generates a meaningful amount of revenue. This is also how a small software startup company like Terminus can self-fund its customer event. Like any media company, the software company sells sponsorships to other non-competitive technology companies that may want to reach Terminus's customer base.

- Build a revenue-generation platform that also drives awareness for a niche business. This is what data and research company Freight-

Waves did in 2016 by launching FreightWaves TV and Freight-Waves radio. It has seen 250 percent growth in both its media and data businesses as a result of launching these new content platforms.

- Create media properties that build valuable audiences to drive funding for other projects. Computer maker Raspberry Pi built a division of its company to publish magazines and books to drive revenue for its foundation that provides low-cost computers for kids.

All these goals are supported by willing, addressable subscribers. But just as these goals vary in scope, so too do their aspirations vis-à-vis their audiences. Put simply, all subscribers are valuable, but they are not equally valuable.

Just as for a media company, the net present value of any audience asset is a snapshot in time. Today, your audience may be small but engaged and willing to take many actions that move it toward your goals. Tomorrow, the audience may be bigger but unengaged and unwilling to help you.

Your goal is to care for the asset as you would any other. You might measure and segment the audience based on its activity. For example, at the Content Marketing Institute we measure unengaged audiences, our fans, and our superfans. We know that superfans spend three times as much for events and other products and services as unengaged audiences. As you might expect, our focus is to convert as many "fans" as we can into "superfans."

As a result, we model subscribers as customers—increasing (or decreasing) in lifetime value on their way to becoming superfans. Today's engaged and active subscriber is tomorrow's disengaged subscriber (or unsubscriber).

While other departments look at increasing customer value by continued purchases over time, content marketers can look at increasing subscriber value as loyalty, activity, depth of relationship, and willingness to take actions over time.

That is something that even a CFO can get behind.

Remember, you can measure both the audiences that meet audience-related goals and audiences that help you achieve more traditional marketing and sales goals.

For example, you can "measure the crosses." If the audience is meant to support a more efficient or effective sales goal, measure the difference between the paths it takes to get there. Put simply, remember our reach and frequency metric. Subscribers are audiences you can more easily (efficiently) reach. Therefore, if they do things faster, better, or in a more valuable way compared with traditional marketing, there is no doubt that there is differential value there.

Some subscribers will cross over into the traditional marketing process. When they do, their value becomes the difference between the cost of acquiring that lead or customer through traditional methods vs. the audience development method.

Again, ServiceNow is a great example. In the first year of *Workflow*'s publication, the company saw 66 percent growth in subscribers. More importantly, subscribers are 73 percent more likely to take the action of completing a lead generation form on the website. Not only does the publication give ServiceNow a more efficient lead generator, but it provides higher-quality customer data when they make a purchase.

And, of course, you can also measure the other path—those who *don't ever* convert into traditional marketing leads and opportunities based on marketing's monetizable goals. Think about how to monetize subscribers or segments of subscribers and assign value based on that.

Remember how Cleveland Clinic monetizes its *Health Essentials* blog? One subscriber segment represents the opportunity for increased local patients (a traditional marketing goal). It's a meaningful but very small percentage of the blog's millions of visitors.

The wider, national segment of "health-conscious" subscribers represents the opportunity for Cleveland Clinic to sell access through advertising from insurance companies, technology companies, and others. But why is this valuable?

Because *Health Essentials* is now a brand and marketing program that provides an incremental number of opportunities for local patients and not only pays for itself through its audience asset but actually generates a profit.

As you reflect on your audience-building approach, what emerges can be both a snapshot of a monetary valuation of the existing subscriber base and a model for new scenarios to increase that value over time.

A great content marketing strategy places the focus on the continual growth of the audience as an asset with many, many attributes. These are people who trust us, engage with us, want to hear from us, and will, over time, exchange value with our business in many ways.

Audiences are the heart of this strategy, so it's fitting that they come at the heart of this book. Before we move to the next chapter, let's take a moment with a story that puts all of these previous chapters into perspective.

The National Multiple Sclerosis Society's content marketing strategy

One of my favorite examples of an organization taking this approach to their content marketing strategy is what the National Multiple Sclerosis Society (NMSS) has been doing over the last couple of years.

Multiple sclerosis is an unpredictable, often disabling disease of the central nervous system. Symptoms range from numbness and tingling to blindness and paralysis, and there is currently no cure for MS. The progress, severity, and specific symptoms of MS in any one person cannot yet be predicted, but advances in research and treatment are leading to better understanding. There are an estimated 1 million people who live with MS in the United States.

To fulfill this mission, the Society funds cutting-edge research, drives change through advocacy, facilitates professional education, collaborates with MS organizations around the world, and provides programs and services designed to help people with MS and their families move forward with their lives.

Ron Zwerin joined the organization as their Executive Vice President of Marketing, Communications, and Brand Strategy in 2018. At the time, the Society was moving from a distributed model—a local chapter-driven organization—to a centralized national organization.

This was a big organizational shift, and his new team of 65 marketers had to shift from primarily focusing on local marketing challenges at the chapter level to a national focus. But, of course, they couldn't forget the local nuances.

Ron decided that the NMSS needed to become an audience-focused organization, driving content marketing and inspiring a national audience to take actions. The entire marketing focus of the organization revolves around getting people involved, whether it's participating in events, learning about research, being involved in the organization, or, of course, donations.

The entire shift for the brand became about how to tell better stories at a national level, and use the scale of the audience to gain insight through all of the data it would produce, which would feed the capability to drive better and more impactful stories that drove even more actions. They began to think about the best ways to restructure their current marketing efforts.

Then, the pandemic hit.

Ron engaged one of the leaders in his marketing effort, Lindsey Read, to create a new content marketing strategy that would become the central focus and enable them to optimize their brand and audience-building efforts.

The first thing they did was to create specific teams with a specific content-oriented set of responsibilities (sound familiar?). They created a growth and acquisitions team to focus on acquiring audiences. They created a constituent experience team to manage the portfolio of digital experiences they would create with content. And they created a content and digital team to start creating the content that fuels those experiences and the operations to make it all cohesive.

Their first test of these new structures and process was to apply their new model against Bike MS, their largest peer-to-peer, coast-to-coast ride to benefit the society. They knew during Covid-19 that the one thing people couldn't do was to get together for a bike ride. So, they creatively decided that they would "digitize the experience." They transformed it into a story of "why you would choose to ride." It's not about technology, it's not about tools, it's not a story of joining a big group. It's a story about why you, as a human, would ride any time, anyplace to benefit a cause like NMSS.

They created multiple experiences with this story, including live shows, rock concerts, and, of course, video and digital experiences. People could ride any time they liked, on their stationary bike, or even just go on a walk.

Then, beyond the one event, the team began to expand the experiences, building an ecosystem of content and operating more like a media company would with connected experiences that would focus on building audiences. As Ron said to me in an interview:

> We started thinking bigger than a website because it's not about a website. It's about the ecosystem. How are we going to get people to engage with us and have a frictionless experience with us as an organization. Whether they come in as a rider, or whether they come in as a volunteer, we know them and can talk to them as though we know them and give them the best experience.

The critical next step for them was to begin doing audience research. They knew from previous experience that they had nine core audiences, and so the key was to understand not what was valuable to them from a "donation" perspective, but what was valuable to them full stop. They employed the classic jobs-to-be-done framework and did both qualitative and quantitative research. And in doing so, they debunked a number of assumptions that they'd held.

For example, they had assumptions that said some people just want to go on the well-known bike rides to benefit MS and that's all they will do. But they discovered that, actually, no. Being a "bike rider" was simply an attribute of people who valued doing many other things.

But, because the organization had siloed "riders," that's the only way they communicated with them. That was the content they received. But now they discovered they should be connecting other experiences to those "riders."

That was when Lindsey and her team began to organize the audiences not by the "nine audiences" that they believed they had, but rather by the jobs-to-be-done framework. This was a way to recognize the multidimensional aspects of people, which evolve over time. They decided to look at their content marketing strategy not as targeting nine different people each with one job, but rather as targeting 14 different jobs that could be part of any one person.

Then they started rank ordering these success statements of the jobs-to-be-done. For example, if they are newly diagnosed with MS, what their journey should be. If they are looking to do Bike MS (be a rider), what is their journey? They then created a beginning, middle, end, and a circle-back framework for all these jobs.

As of the writing of this book, the organization is beginning to implement this new way of looking at audiences and their content marketing strategy and beginning to build out the coordinated communication between the teams, the content operations, and ultimately the connected experiences that will bring this all together.

They have even begun to add these jobs as the goals for all of the cross-functional teams. And they have started to map that against one of the more unique business goals of all time.

They want to end the organization.

As Ron said to me in our interview, "The organization is 70 years old, and we are at a point now where we need to start thinking about the endgame here. So, our job is not to do this for 50 more years. If we end this organization, it's because we've cured MS. That is where our sights are set now."

That sets our sights on our next chapter, which is building our content.

Notes

1 Drucker, P.F. (1975) *The Practice of Management*, Allied Publishers, p.37

2 Napoli, P.M. (2003) *Audience Economics: Media institutions and the audience marketplace*, New York: Columbia University Press, p.3

3 Pulizzi, J. (2014) *Epic Content Marketing: How to tell a different story, break through the clutter, and win more customers by marketing less*, New York: McGraw-Hill Education, p.126

4 Gyn, A. (2022) How'd you make that flipping awesome B2B content for ServiceNow? Content Marketing Institute, https://contentmarketinginstitute.com/articles/b2b-award-winning-content-servicenow (archived at https://perma.cc/ZK6K-VCXY)

The Product Management of Content

Creating Differentiating Content Marketing

Don't just create a content strategy for the business, create a whole business strategy for the content.

Okay, so now we know our audience. But it's time we asked the question, who are we? What are content marketers, *really*?

You may have noticed something about most of the examples of content marketing in this book, and just about every successful content marketing strategy you'll hear about: They aren't projects or campaigns.

The magazine *Ad Age* (known as *Advertising Age* until 2017) has covered the world of marketing and advertising since 1930. It is, perhaps, the most iconic of all the marketing industry publications. One of the magazine's main focuses is to cover creative and innovative marketing and advertising campaigns. In fact, the *Ad Age* website now has an entire "Creativity" section that is nothing but coverage of what it considers to be the best recent campaigns by mainstream brands. Each article provides a book report-style outline of the creativity and the strategy behind it, down to a Hollywood-style credits section listing all the various skill players who contributed to it.

But I've never seen a content marketing effort in any of their lists. Why is that?

It is because successful content marketing isn't a short-term campaign. As discussed in previous chapters, it's an integrated operation that feeds into all of the marketing, advertising, customer service, and loyalty efforts that are being done.

Content marketing is a marketing-led set of activities, but it is a *business* strategy.

That's not to say that content marketing cannot exist tactically within a traditional campaign. In fact, as we've discussed, that is how many content marketing strategies begin. It might be as simple as one "how-to" ebook that is used as the bait for an advertising campaign. Have you ever seen one of those late-night television advertisements that, at the end, promise a "free educational guide" to help you understand whatever complex issue it is they're selling? Or, using an approach called "advertorial," you might pay for a full-page ad in a magazine. However, you might design that "ad" to look just like a feature article from the magazine—complete with valuable information and a byline. In its simplest state, both of these examples are content marketing existing within a traditional marketing campaign.

However, most successful content marketing efforts at some point go beyond that producer model of simply providing digital assets as bait for paid media campaigns. They add the approaches in the Product and/or Platform quadrant to develop owned media experiences. Why? Because as we learned in the last chapter, the key to a great content marketing strategy is an engaged, subscribed audience asset. That is what enables the exponential success and how content marketing adds wealth to our business. Thus, we must *become the media* that our audience wants to interact with over the long term. We must create not just one valuable asset, but owned media experiences that continue to service a subscribed audience in an ongoing fashion.

So, what does "owned media experiences" really mean?

From the previous chapters, we now understand that content marketing is best served as a media operation, and thus its business value as an approach is built upon attracting an engaged, loyal audience that can be monetized over time.

It's the "over time" part of that sentence that is important. Building an audience isn't possible in a one-and-done campaign. Therefore, it makes sense that most of the really successful examples of content marketing strategy are not one-off white papers, campaigns, or 30-second TV spots. Rather, they tend to be in-depth publications, original research efforts, episodic series, newsletters, thought leadership resource centers, learning platforms, and other types of content-driven experiences.

In two words: media products.

You will also remember that I began this book by illustrating the three pillars of a content marketing strategy. One of those pillars is coordinating the content (the ingredients). The second is the operation (the process and standards) of how those ingredients can be consistently sourced and mixed. And the third is the "experiences" (the content products) that are the culmination of the recipes that contain those ingredients.

Also remember that in Chapter 5 we turned our attention outward and looked at broader audiences—a more expansive view of our customer. We began to understand how we would identify their needs and wants first, to expand the ideas and value we could deliver through content. The story of the National Multiple Sclerosis Society ended with their focus on beginning to build their portfolio of experiences that would deliver on the promise of helping all of those jobs-to-be-done from their various audiences.

Putting all that together, doesn't it sound an awful lot like a strategy to build new products?

Content marketers are ultimately product managers, helping to understand the needs of a market (the audience) and improve business value by developing and distributing media products that meet those needs. By optimizing the activities to understand how *all* content flows through marketing, we can then balance our team's charter to make room for leading the activity to actually develop those products.

So, if content marketers are really media product managers, and we've now balanced our responsibilities to give our teams a capacity to build something, where do we begin to develop the product of content?

The answer is fairly obvious: As with most products, we start with *our* idea.

Here's a little secret that is true for most businesses but doesn't get discussed often. As much as we'd all like to believe that the most brilliant new products come from deep, contemplative thought and research and ascertaining what potential customers need and want, the simple truth is that most don't. Most are either iterations of something that's already out in the marketplace (we can make it better, faster, or cheaper), or they really are new and innovative but, by definition, have little to do with what customers have identified as missing in their lives.

No one *needed or was asking for* a Rubik's Cube, an iPhone, Michael Jackson's *Thriller* album, or a Toyota Corolla. The reason that these four products are among the top 10 bestselling products in history isn't that someone went out and asked customers "What is missing about your mobile phone needs?" or "What kind of 3D puzzles would be the most compelling for you?" or "What should Michael Jackson's next album be about?" No. The reason that these products and so many others succeed is because someone sees something that's not there—something that will work better (be more compelling) for a customer—and they also have a vision for how to bring that something to reality. The most important thing to remember is that the order of those two reasons matters a lot.

There is a wonderful video of Apple founder Steve Jobs from 1997. For context, remember Jobs had just returned to Apple, after having been fired 10 years earlier. This was his first appearance at Apple's Worldwide Developer's Conference since returning to the company. He was taking questions from the audience, when one developer took him to task about product development. The questioner asked a relatively technical question about why Jobs was killing a particular product. But the implication was bigger than that. One of the first things Jobs did upon his return was to reduce the number of products that Apple made by 70 percent.[1] Jobs didn't answer the question he was asked, but he answered the larger question by saying:

> One of the things that I've always found is that you've got to start with the customer experience and work backwards to the technology. You can't start with the technology and try to figure out where you're going to try and sell it.[2]

Jobs knew then that you start by having a vision of the experience that you want the customer to have. Then, you work backwards to figuring out what it is you need to build.

This same guiding light is true for our content creation as well. Think about that. Pause for a moment and think about the list of products I mentioned. Did any of them stand out to you? Perhaps the Michael Jackson album seemed different. It is, indeed, the highest-selling album of all time, with, to date, sales of over 70 million copies worldwide. But surely, Jackson, as a content creator, didn't start that process thinking about what "gaps" there were in the marketplace before he started writing songs for *Thriller*. Probably not. But I guarantee you CBS Records (Jackson's record company at the time) did. In fact, the effort they put around the, then new, idea of using highly produced music videos, and making what was the most expensive (and longest) video of its time, is not only a great example of content marketing, it's the way that the marketing team found a huge gap in the marketplace that would be filled with the music of *Thriller*. You see, what Michael Jackson's team didn't do was to start with a finished product and try to sell it like every other album that had come before by claiming that the differentiator was that "*it's Michael Jackson.*" No. They started with the experience that they believed would be desired, and then worked backward to see how to sell the product.

Starting development of any kind of content with *our* idea of what is valuable is just natural for humans. We may get an idea by observing a gap in the marketplace, but we mostly start our process from what *we believe* will be the most valuable to fill that need. This approach is almost a prerequisite when we're thinking about it from a marketing perspective. Think about it—if our new team is going to produce some awesome new content product that will serve the business's purpose, you can be sure that we should be doing this in lock-step alignment with whatever the company's current mission and objectives already are. We get so wrapped up in our brand and what we're trying to sell, that we limit our ideas to only the thing we're trying to sell. Is it any wonder that most companies' blogs, social media channels, or online resource centers are just glorified brochures, talking about the product?

It's like being on a date with someone who can't stop talking, but they finally realize they haven't let you get a word in edgewise and say to you, "Enough about me, what do you think about me?"

Our first step is to understand "why" our content should exist. And, spoiler alert, it's not about our "why."

Whose "why" is first?

One of the most popular business marketing theories to emerge in the last decade is to "know your why." The phrase is now so popular that it's almost become a bit of a marketing cliché.

But this advice often steers both product managers and content marketers wrong.

The idea of finding the "why" behind what you do caught on almost a dozen years ago due to Simon Sinek's book (and accompanying TED Talk), *Start With Why*.

From a product marketing and brand lens, Sinek's idea was simple. "People don't buy what you do; they buy why you do it," he claimed. Therefore, he suggested, brands should start their positioning for their product idea with their "why."[3]

It has become a core staple of brand positioning since.

Sinek pulled back from the brand-positioning "why" in his second book (*Find Your Why: A practical guide for discovering purpose for you and your team*), focusing instead on how people can find their own unique purpose to motivate their actions in life.[4]

I believe this is the much more useful purpose for his "why" framework.

But the first approach stuck—finding the brand's "why" for its idea before creating content. Now it is often the rallying cry of agencies and consultants in their approaches to harnessing a bigger brand story.

Here's the problem: Most likely, no one outside your brand cares about your brand's "why."

The challenge of my "why"-based content

Let's be honest. Most businesses don't start with (or stick with) some fantastic, world-changing "why." Remember, their original product idea probably didn't even start with the customer. In fact, this is one of the biggest pushbacks on the "why" idea that I hear from companies that are thinking of starting a content marketing strategy and have been asked by some agency to retrofit a business "why."

They'll say, "Look, we don't offer cute pets, or sexy fashion, or cool gadgets. Our brand and products are all about [insert something boring like rain gutters, or lab equipment, or industrial generators]. What's our world-changing 'why'?" They're not wrong. It's much easier to come up with a "why" that tugs at your heart when it fits neatly into a conventional emotional box.

Even some of Sinek's original examples evolved from this approach. For example, his 2009 TEDx Talk, which now has more than 60 million views, opened with his interpretation of Apple Computer's "why" as a success story. He said that Apple might say, "In everything we do, we believe in challenging the status quo. We believe in thinking differently."[5]

That's nice, it aligns nicely with some of Apple's marketing content, and it certainly is broad enough to be "true-ish." But it's certainly not Apple's past or present "why." Put simply: For any brand it's much easier to superimpose a "why" based on success of any one campaign, and then work backward and point to it in the content, than it is to start with a "why" and transpose it into all content going forward for a long-term mission.

Sinek's "why" statement for Apple was almost certainly inspired by Apple's very successful and quite famous (and covered extensively in *Ad Age*) "Think Different" campaign, which ran from 1997 to 2002.

By the time Sinek was writing his book and giving his TEDx Talk in 2009, Apple was entirely focused on the "Get a Mac" campaign. These commercials featured comedian John Hodgman personifying a PC and actor Justin Long as a Mac talking about how Apple's platform made things like creating photobooks and listening to music easier. Instead of focusing on Apple's "why," the ads explain how the product's features connect to why potential customers would want it.

Even in the last five years, Apple has had numerous marketing campaigns, none of them nearly as iconic as the "Think Different" campaign. Not one has been designed from a brand "why" of "challenging the status quo" as the heart of their entire business.

Apple didn't create or discover its "why" and then decide to change its business to match it. No. Apple continually re-evaluates its *customer's* "why" for its products. Then it clarifies *what* the story should be and evolves its business and how to communicate it. Apple's iconic brand values then provide a prism on *how* any brand story is told.

Understand your customer's "why"

Understanding your brand's "why" is important. It's the mission that motivates, inspires, and provides the initial backbone for the business and a common philosophy for the employees. But (not to get too meta here) understanding your customer's "why" matters much, much more for both marketing campaigns *and* content marketing strategy development.

This is why understanding all the jobs-to-be-done from the previous chapter is so critical to developing your content marketing strategy. If you are to develop content products, you will need to connect some or all of your brand, products, and services to whatever idea you have for a content platform.

In any business, it matters not how boring the actual subject is. You can be successful in developing a content product if you understand your customer's "why"—whether or not you understand your own. Understanding both is nice, but understanding why your customers care is infinitely more important.

Quick side story: I once sat down with a vice president of marketing at one of the largest companies in the semiconductor industry. As I was sitting in their office, I asked about the products they put into the marketplace. The VP stood up, opened a drawer, reached in and carefully fished something out. He said, "Open up your hand." I did, and he dropped what looked like a tiny checkerboard into it. It was black, with little gold squares etched into it. He said: "There you go. Think we can make that sexy with content?"

I said, "Maybe—what does it do?" He said, "Pick up your phone." I did. He paused for a moment and then asked, "Did it light up and work?" I said, "Yeah, it did." He grinned and replied: "That's what it does. It's kinda important."

It doesn't matter if your product is the coolest new fashionable tech gadget, the fluffiest new pet, or a boring set of rain gutters or industrial generators. If the product sells, it delivers value, and that value—or the customer's "why"—is the most important thing you have to understand.

I've personally seen many startup entrepreneurs who have a terrifically clear brand "why" around how they want to save humanity, or think differently, or have some new disruptive point of view about how the world works. These same entrepreneurs are confused when the reactions to their "whys" are returned with the question, "Do customers care about any of that?" Your product/brand doesn't matter if people don't understand why they want or need what you offer.

Does that mean you shouldn't care about your brand's "why"? No, of course you should care. But one reason marketers struggle to create content marketing that truly differentiates and harnesses the power of the brand voice is *not* that they don't understand how to discover their "why." It's that they believe the brand's "why" should dictate everything they do.

For example, I'll often ask a marketing practitioner what they would like their content marketing effort to be, and they'll say something like, "We need people to understand that we're a thought leader in our industry," or "We want customers to align with the fact that we care about the planet." My response to that is to tell them that exactly zero people on the planet need to understand that they are a thought leader. No one's day will be ruined by not understanding or knowing that your brand is trying to do good things for the planet. Nobody on Earth will wake up and say, "Boy, you know what's really missing from my life, Brand X demonstrating that they are thought leaders in my industry and that they care about the planet."

Your brand's "why" should define why you do what you do and how it connects to things customers care about. In other words, you still must convince customers to love what you do and how you do it.

This leads us to the first (really the second) step in the content product development process. The actual first step was to work on understanding your audience persona and their "so I can"—their jobs-to-be-done. Now, you're ready. You've built a team that has a focused charter to create content marketing at scale. You understand how to coordinate your content in a standardized way. And you've begun to research your audiences to understand some of the things they may care about.

Now you're ready to start designing that first media product experience.

Step 1: Understand your audience and their jobs-to-be-done

The good news is if you've gone through Chapter 5, you've already begun the first step. And so you're already prepared to move forward.

Step 2: Focus on the customer's journey

If I'm honest, this step is what most people expect the beginning of a content marketing strategy to be. It's very common that when I'm called in as a consultant, it's because a marketing team has an idea about doing a new blog, podcast, magazine, resource center, or some other cool new content marketing initiative and the question to me is, "Where do we start?"

I immediately spoil all the excitement by asking about team charters, and process, and governance, and if they've done their audience persona work. Yes, we need to do all that work first. Unfortunately, great content product ideas usually end up as short campaigns that die as quickly as the next unexpected priority appears.

Here's an interesting statistic for you. Spotify has more than four million podcasts on its platform. Apple has more than two million. Recent research shows that less than 4 percent of Spotify's four million podcasts have more than 10 episodes. Almost half (47 percent) have three or fewer episodes.[6] The lesson is, just like products in the real world, exceedingly few podcasts succeed over the long term—and most die not because of consumer disinterest but from lack of commitment from the product creators.

While this may seem like great news for any marketing team that wants to launch a podcast (less competition than we think), the reality is that this is a great representation of why content marketing products are fraught with failure. If you don't do the prerequisite work to figure out your team, the charter, your governance, and your audience, you will almost certainly not prioritize the activity of a long-term commitment to your content marketing product.

But at some point we do begin to talk about development of the content marketing product, and my preferred place is to start by connecting the audience's job-to-be-done (the valuable experience) with whatever the business objective will be for this new product.

Put simply: Let's identify where this new experience/product will sit on the customer's journey.

We begin with the infinity loop version of a customer's journey. This is an optimal way to plot where you already have content experiences that may need to be optimized or where there may be obvious gaps to fill.

Figure 6.1   The Customer's Journey

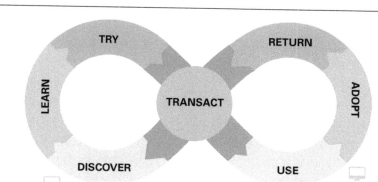

NOTE The customer's journey begins in the lower left and then goes clockwise through the Learn, Try, and Transact phases, before circling back through the Use (Onboarding), Adopt (Loyalty) and Return (Upsell, Cross-Sell) phases.

You will see that I've segmented each part of the journey into a high-level, seven-step process that maps to marketing's business objectives. Now, your customer's journey may be different, and probably will be. But these seven steps are generally as follows:

1 **Discover:** where your business objective is all about reach and frequency. This is where the content is driving awareness programs about new or existing products or a particular point of view it wants to share. This is the world of brand campaigns, awareness initiatives, and demand generation. If you can drive action at this stage, it leads to...

2 **Learn:** where you hope that potential customers are interested enough to learn more about the thing you offer. Here your hope is to drive inquiries, and discussions, where aware audiences become interested leads. The marketer's job here is to educate, engage, entertain, or in some way create high degrees of interest so that interest in learning leads to...

3 **Try:** where the interested lead becomes an opportunity, or potential customer. This is the stage of "demonstrated value." With a highly considered purchase such as an automobile or home, this is where the potential customer takes a test drive or tours the home. In a B2B setting, this may be the stage where samples are sent, or demonstrations are performed. In a high-velocity transaction environment such as a grocery store or e-commerce site, this is where the individual has placed items in their shopping cart. Successful sales and marketing here lead to...

4 **Transact:** a focal point of the customer's journey, because in some instances this is where the marketing team's responsibility may end. But, as we discussed, creating a transaction with a customer doesn't necessarily mean you've created a true, valuable customer. In many cases, businesses offer loss-leaders, or deep discounts, or even "free trials" that will convert into wealth for the business if they can keep that customer engaged for a longer period. Regardless, even if marketing's responsibilities end at the transaction, content marketing activities extend well into the next step, which is...

5 **Use:** where you design onboarding, instructional, or helpful experiences designed to teach your customers to be better customers.

This is the stage of the instruction manual or the online community to train your customers. This is where customer satisfaction is built and is focused on your ability to reduce friction and help your customer get the most out of what they have transacted with you. If you are successful at this stage, then the customer will move into...

6 **Adopt:** where the customer has integrated the value provided at the transact and use stages and has made that value part of themselves. If you are successful here, this is the evangelizing stage, where customers provide great reviews or spread the word to friends, family, or colleagues about the success they've had with the value they received from you. This is the stage for great customer stories and shared experiences. It's also the place for adding products, services, or partner services to entice these happy people to explore learning about what more they can do with your brand. If you are successful here, that leads to the final step, which brings everything around to...

7 **Return:** where you see a stage similar to the "try" experience, but this time you have permission to expand and/or deepen your relationship. If you are successful here, you have demonstrated long-term value and the customer's relationship with you is trusted enough to be willing to consider re-purchasing, re-subscribing, or widening their relationship with you to different types of value. This is where your opportunity to expand or deepen your relationship with the customer is at its highest. And, if you are successful at convincing them to transact again, it brings a loyalty to the brand that brings you all the way back around to an opportunity to make them aware any time you have something new.

Suffice it to say that for every successful trip around the customer journey loop, the customer moves from stage to stage more easily.

With these stages in mind—as well as your purpose, responsibilities, and audience research—your task is to identify where your new content product will sit along this journey.

Now, the first reaction may be, "Well, we should build an experience that covers more than one stage." We'll get to that, and even allow for it, but just be aware that the more areas a business tries to cover, the less effective the content product tends to be. In other words, if you're trying to build a publication that helps to drive awareness and also create a helpful onboarding experience for new customers, it's probably not going to fare nearly as well as if you focus on one or the other.

So, to start, pick one.

For example, in Chapter 3 I told you about Cleveland Clinic's *Health Essentials* publication. This is absolutely a focused "discover" experience. It is designed specifically to share insight into better, healthier ways to live. The objective is to drive broad awareness of best practices in health so that more and more people might come to associate Cleveland Clinic with the best in modern practices for proactive healthcare. While there are definitely calls to action such as "subscribe to our newsletter," there are no "find a doctor" links on this site, or any lead generation activity at all. At most, you may find links to their Health Library site, which is a great example of a "learn" experience.

REI, the sporting goods company, provides another example of having a different purpose for a content product. Their Expert Advice blogs contain "buying advice" and "gear guides" that help buyers understand what products the experts believe will go well with the other things they are considering. It is a great example of a "try" experience, where these guides serve as a consultative, helpful sales expert not there to pressure customers but to educate them on additional products they may want to add to their shopping cart.

A final example of a very focused content marketing effort is Peloton and their Peloton Studios. The company launched this entire division to focus on "adopt" experiences, where the company creates valuable content designed to encourage the customer to keep using their bike, treadmill, or other equipment.

Picking a step in the journey where your new content product fits provides it with a purpose. It helps to define the objectives and measurement approaches that we will cover in Chapter 8.

Now you can begin to refine that purpose with a focused set of initial objectives for your new content product.

Step 3: Choose a focus value

The next step in defining your new product is to choose where you will want to guide the customer to the "best next" experience. In other words, what focused action do you want to inspire in the audience after they consume this content. As you might expect, different categories of value span the customer's journey. Misalignment in purpose and focus is the most common reason that a new content marketing product fails for a business.

For example, we will often see that a new "discover"-oriented blog or resource center is expected to drive nurtured leads to a sales process. So, success is measured by how many sales an awareness-focused publication is driving. This almost always ends up in disappointment.

Think of it this way. If Cleveland Clinic measured their *Health Essentials* blog by how many inquiries came into their "find the right doctor" form, their blog would be a failure. The content is all squarely focused on helping people be proactive about their healthcare. Therefore, their engaged and subscribed audiences aren't looking for a doctor yet. These are audiences that seek better ways to take care of themselves. That's the job-to-be-done in this case. Measuring it by how many people are signing up to see a doctor would be silly.

Yet, this is the way many new content marketing projects are started. So, once you have decided which step in the customer's journey will best serve your business goals, it's time to select a focus value.

In my experience, there are seven categories of clear focus that can help you define where and how your content marketing product will be successful.

These are the categories:

1 **Inspire Conversation.** In the earliest parts of the awareness challenge, your only focus may be to inspire conversation so that more and more people are aware of you or your point of view in the marketplace. This focus is especially common for new, disruptive businesses introducing new concepts to the world. A great example of this is the podcast I have with my colleague, Joe Pulizzi. We launched This Old Marketing in 2013 to drive interest

Figure 6.2 The Customer's Journey With Focused Objectives

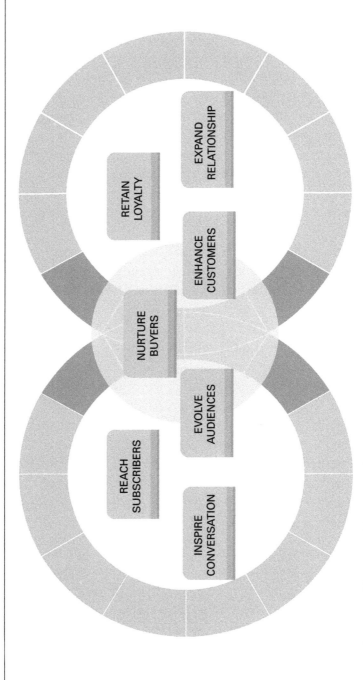

NOTE Each segment of the customer's journey provides opportunity for focused objectives for content marketing. One or a few of these can provide the focus you need for a content product.

in the concept of content marketing. Our goal wasn't to drive leads or subscribers to anything. It was simply to evangelize the concepts of content marketing so that people might get interested enough to want to learn more. We measured ourselves by how many people we reached (how many people listen), how much traffic we drew to the Content Marketing Institute website, and how many people talked about the show on social media.

2 **Reach Subscribers.** As you move further into the customer's journey, it becomes important to be able to reach audiences at your discretion. As Chapter 5 discussed, subscribed audiences are one of the best ways to start to monetize audiences in different ways. So, your next focus might be to drive aware, known subscribers who match your target to your content product.

3 **Evolve Audiences.** As you deepen your relationship with those audiences either in the short or long term, your goal may be to evolve them as "leads" or "interested" in your products and services. The focus may be to educate them on a particular concept that would lead them to become customers. A great example is what HubSpot did with the concept of inbound marketing. HubSpot created an entire content program (including a book, multiple blogs, and even an event) designed to teach people the concept of inbound marketing, all with the hope of driving them to discover that HubSpot software was a perfect candidate to solve this new approach to marketing.

4 **Nurture Buyers.** As your customer approaches the "transact" stage, a common focus for your content marketing product may be to help nurture prospective customers into becoming higher-value transactions. It may be, as with REI's Expert Advice blog, a means of helping customers add more related gear to their purchase. Or, in the case of a B2B-focused effort, it may be to show through education and demonstrations how "straightforward" the implementation of a new product will be once the buyer has approved the sale.

5 **Enhance Customers.** Once the transaction is complete, your eye turns toward helping customers utilize the thing they have just acquired. Here a helpful education program or a "how-to" library becomes focused on enhancing customers and transforming them

into long-term, satisfied customers. I like to call this the focus where you teach customers how to be better customers.

6 **Retain Loyalty.** As you move into the "adopt" and "return" stages of the customer's journey, your focus may turn to loyalty and evangelism. Here your focus is to use a content marketing product to drive deeper involvement with your brand, or to drive shareable stories where members of your subscribed audience become "superfans" of your brand and the products and services you have provided.

7 **Expand Relationships.** Finally, as you circle back around, your opportunity is to expand your relationship with your customer audience. You can add expanded value to their lives that helps expand your relationship or add to the relationship in a way that encourages them to remain, or recur, as customers. A great example is Salesforce and their Dreamforce event. This event has become one of the biggest technology-focused industry events on the planet. The reported in-person attendance at the 2022 event was 40,000. This is much lower than pre-pandemic numbers, like the 150,000 who reportedly attended in 2019, but still makes it one of the largest events of its kind. While there are product education sessions scheduled for customers, the biggest draw are the concerts by bands such as Red Hot Chili Peppers and celebrity keynote speakers such as singer Jennifer Hudson, actor Matthew McConaughey, former vice president Al Gore, and Olympic gymnast Simone Biles. It is Salesforce's drive to provide not just great software, but also once-in-a-lifetime celebration events that keep you returning as a Salesforce customer.

Your chosen focus aligns with your purpose, and both help to determine the editorial strategy and everything that will help you drive the clearest content marketing product development plan.

Step 4: Begin to assemble the product plan

You'll remember we started this process at Step 2. That was because Step 1 was to identify your audience, from the previous chapter. Now, you might get lucky and have your process work just in that order.

However, as we discussed at the beginning of this chapter, it's rare that we can look at the audience's needs and then design a product to match.

It's much more common to start from the point where the team has an idea for a content marketing experience and wants to know how to build it.

In either case, the key is to work on four elements together:

- **Pick your purpose(s).** What is the experiential purpose for your new content marketing product? Where will it sit in the customer's journey? This is how we connect the audience's "why" with the business objectives. I mentioned earlier in this chapter that you can allow for more than one purpose. There are instances where you may want the experience to act as a bit of a bridge. For example, you may want a content marketing product that is primarily a "learn" experience but also helps interested audiences see the demonstrated value as a "try" experience. Or you may see an opportunity to create a how-to "use" experience that doubles as a customer community "adopt" experience. You may even convince me that there's room to cover three or four purposes with one content experience. Trust me, I'll fight that idea vigorously, but this is your strategy and these are your decisions.

- **Choose your focuses.** Unlike purposes, you are likely to have more than one focus, especially as you scale and grow your content marketing product. It's common to both inspire conversation and reach subscribers, for example. This is arguably what Cleveland Clinic's *Health Essentials* blog is really focused on. The key is that your focuses are aligned with your purpose(s), and they are adjacent to one another. For example, it would be a mistake to choose "inspire conversation" and "retain loyalty" because these are not adjacent. That is a chosen set of focuses that I would disagree with. But again, these are your decisions.

- **Identify your audience.** Based on any of these other three decisions, this may have been the first thing you did, or it may be the last thing. You may decide that you have the perfect idea, with the right purpose and focus, and you just need to go validate an audience for this new thing. Or you may decide that you have the perfect audience and you need to fill out the rest of this through deeper or more intricate audience research. Either way, document and include your chosen audience and success statements in this content product plan.

- **Highlight your idea.** You may have a full 10-page description of your idea, or simply one sentence. The next chapter explores how to get to deeper storytelling value, but for now you can detail what's "in" and what's "out." For example, you may simply decide that it's an educational publication featuring great how-to content. Ask yourself, if it were a media company what would it be, and how will it be different than what's in the marketplace already?

If you're looking for some great examples of content marketing product plans, we've got you covered. They are available at ContentMarketingStrategy.com

---

Your product plan is ready for detail now. And if you're like most product managers, you'll come to love this part of the process the most. It's the part of the content marketing strategy where you get to focus on building interesting things.

You've probably heard the advice: "Do what you love. The money will follow." Most people take this to mean that if we're simply passionate about why we're doing something, the world will ultimately find value in it as well. It's really the corollary to why it's important to understand your own "why."

But for content creators and marketers working for a brand, I suggest this tweak: "When your audience loves what you love to do, the money will follow."

Matching your brand's "why" to your audience's and customer's "why" sets you on the path to convincing them to love what you love to do. And that's how your brand will find success in whatever it loves to do.

Notes

1 Fell, J. (2011) How Steve Jobs saved Apple, *Entrepreneur*, https://www.
   entrepreneur.com/growing-a-business/how-steve-jobs-saved-apple/220604
   (archived at https://perma.cc/6LY5-77PB)
2 Steve Jobs customer experience (2015) YouTube, https://www.youtube.
   com/watch?v=r2O5qKZlI50 (archived at https://perma.cc/36MN-6W45)
3 Sinek, S., Mead, D., and Docker, P. (2017) *Find Your Why: A practical
   guide for discovering purpose for you and your team*, New York:
   Portfolio / Penguin
4 Ibid
5 Sinek, S. (2009) How great leaders inspire action, Ted.com, https://www.
   ted.com/talks/simon_sinek_how_great_leaders_inspire_action?language=en
   (archived at https://perma.cc/J7XZ-CXFX)
6 Goldstein, S. (2021) A surprisingly small number of podcasts are still in
   production, amplifi media, https://www.amplifimedia.com/blogstein-1/ly
   spqop3ylro9a2t7y2de820uwkgwx?rq=3%20or%20fewer%20episodes
   (archived at https://perma.cc/6WQM-Z3WU)

Finding Story   07

Structure Your Story Before You Create the Content

It's your story. Tell it well.

What should we talk about?

When the publisher of this book and I started talking about possible subtitles, we went round and round on a few versions. The purpose of a great subtitle is, of course, to provide context to the title—which is supposed to summarize the book in as few words as possible.

Ultimately, we came to what you see on the cover: "Harness the Power of Your Brand's Voice."

"Harness" felt like a good word because we all tell stories, and as you can hopefully intuit by this point in the book, a content marketing strategy is much more about how we collaborate and get our arms around consistent communication than about how to create the stories.

But perhaps the most important element of that subtitle is the simple little apostrophe. It assumes that every brand has a voice—and that while that voice belongs to the brand, the stories it tells may not be *about* the brand.

But let's back up a moment to a concept called storytelling. It's got a bit of a buzz these days, hasn't it?

It seems every technology provider, agency, and consultant promises to help you tell a better story. But what does "telling a better story" even mean?

To tell a better story, do marketers need to be edgier and differentiate themselves to an audience numb to everything except the completely outrageous? Does every piece of content have to look like a Super Bowl commercial? Maybe. But doesn't that ultimately seem like a zero-sum game? How many more over-the-top content ideas do you produce before you jump the proverbial shark?

And today's mainstream news headlines are probably going to be more outrageous than your brand will ever be able to muster, anyway.

Does "telling a better story" mean you need to put more and more detail into your content? Give away all the thinking and bombard your audience with so much quality and detailed information (#AllTheEducation) that they must appreciate the sheer amount of content?

No. Neither of these approaches is at the root of getting to a better story.

I spent much of my early career on a deep dive into the theory behind "story." My adventures (some might say misadventures) as a playwright and screenwriter gave me access to some of the best teachers in the world of storytelling, many of whom drilled this into my head: At the heart of a great story is an *argument for a truth*. And truth has little to do with the number of facts or what happens, no matter how outrageous.

One of my mentors—the great storytelling coach Robert McKee—has written, "What happens is fact, not truth. Truth is what we *think* about what happens."[1] In other words, we believe that what happened matters. We care.

This is one of the reasons that artificial intelligence is still a long way from becoming a threat to great storytelling. AI is wonderful at writing plot; it can lay out *what happened* in well-constructed and detailed sentences. But what it can't do (yet) is creatively pull through themes and construct what happened in a way that illuminates some new, universal truth.

For example, if you ask artificial intelligence to tell you the story of the original *Star Wars* movie (and I did exactly that), you'll get something like the following:

> It is an epic tale of civil war between the evil Galactic Empire, led by
> Emperor Palpatine, and the heroic Rebel Alliance, led by Princess Leia

and other freedom fighters. The central characters in the story are Luke Skywalker, Han Solo, Chewbacca, and R2-D2. Together, these heroes must face up against the formidable evil forces of Darth Vader, the Imperial Military, and their monstrous armada.[2]

Of course, aside from the glaring omission of C3PO, that's a wonderfully impressive description of the plot: what happens. But if you hadn't seen *Star Wars*, would that story make you care?

The story of *Star Wars* is, of course, much different. It is about a young farm boy who longs for more meaning and adventure in his life, then discovers that it is not heroics but his faith in his friends and a force bigger than himself that provide the true meaning in life.

Now, that's one take on an illuminated truth coming out of a story. You may have another. The point is that the difference between plot and story is this: Story will ultimately make someone care about a universal truth.

Put simply, a great story is a well-crafted, entertaining, engaging, and (ultimately) convincing argument. With a fulfilling story, if I'm successful as an author I've taken you on a journey and you believe (or are at least open to believing) something different at the end of it.

The struggle for business stories

But, okay, that's Hollywood. Are we really telling stories in marketing and business?

When we work with companies, both large and small, one common trend is that marketers have locked themselves into their brand messaging. This is not surprising, because one of the first things any business tries to do is lock down its brand message, its main value proposition. Whether it's a "start with why" perspective or a new "brand messaging platform," content marketers are usually not starting from scratch. They are working within a well-established—if not well-formulated—set of rules about what, where, how, and when to create content that represents the company's positioning of its brand and products.

There are clear value propositions and differentiators. The teams understand the paid media schedule. The agency is working out creative advertising and brochure elements, and the PR team is readying news around new hires, products, and partnerships.

The content marketing team, however, is struggling with individual topics that fit within this new or existing platform. So, they meet with the other groups. Here's how that usually goes:

- Someone from the demand generation team suggests creating a list of all the questions buyers might ask about the company's particular approach.

- The product marketing manager likes that idea and says, "We could create articles answering those questions and then sprinkle in how we solve those challenges."

- The brand marketing manager says, "Why don't we write some posts about our new brand mission and how our products and services are helping solve climate change?" They punctuate their suggestion by throwing a copy of Simon Sinek's *Start With Why* onto the table.

- The product marketing manager chimes in: "Yes, and we could sprinkle in a bit about how our product solves those challenges."

- "I know," says someone from PR, "let's write posts that feature profiles of our executives and their thought leadership in the market."

- The brand marketing manager nods in appreciation. "Yes, great idea. That's storytelling. It's got a hero."

- The product marketing manager stands up and says, "I like it. And maybe the executives could talk a little about how our product solves difficult challenges."

- Only the content marketing team sit silently, looking down at their notebooks. They've taken exactly zero notes.

- The pizza arrives, and the meeting ends. The brand marketing manager says, "I don't know what you were all so worried about. We've got tons of things to talk about."

Let's try a different approach.

Your brand's stories?

One of the more controversial topics in marketing is how much control any company has over its "brand." On one side are those who say brand control is an illusion. They say you have no control—and never did—over how your brand is perceived.

Then there are the articles, services, templates, books, and other resources that aim to help companies build a strong and powerful brand identity. Whether it's seven principles, 11 steps, five proven ways, or how to build it in five days—it seems as if everyone has a take on how to do it.

Can both arguments be correct?

In my experience, they are. Marketers *do* set out to distinguish their brands and demonstrate that distinction through creative visuals, messages, voice, and the experiences they create for prospective customers.

But when there's a conflict between what you say your brand stands for and both the content-driven experiences you create and the product or service you offer to the marketplace, you lose control of your brand perception.

In other words, you can create a slick logo, a tagline, and guidelines that aim to set your brand apart. But if you fail to deliver with either the product or service or any of the content experiences you create, then consumers will start to distinguish the brand in their own way.

And, unfortunately, it's rarely an interpretation that you'd prefer.

Nowhere does this phenomenon play a bigger role today than in the content we create: the brand story and the brand's stories. Yes, there is a difference. The apostrophe matters.

You see, when marketing teams talk about telling a "brand story," such as in the scene I laid out at the beginning of this chapter, they're usually discussing the story the brand's leaders tell about the brand itself. And then they quickly run into a dead end.

But the brand story is different from the brand's stories—namely the content marketing stories you are going to create to support the brand.

Enough about me—tell me a story about me

The first reason content marketers struggle with the brand's stories is that the brand's values usually aren't anything that can be used as the foundation of the story. Setting aside the brand symbol/logo, taglines, and core visuals, you're left with value statements that the company believes to be true *about itself*.

For example, look at a Nike brand value statement:

> [Nike] brings inspiration and innovation to every athlete in the world and if you have a body, you are an athlete.[3]

That's good stuff, and very helpful if you're trying to understand how the Nike brand sees itself in contrast to others that sell sportswear. But for a Nike marketer looking to create a new fulfilling story experience within the brand, it's as the old English proverb says: "Fine words butter no parsnips."

In short, an audience looking for stories won't find these words terribly helpful, because the ideal already is fulfilled. There's no journey to go on. It's very much like how the content marketers felt in the meeting with all the other groups. Everybody had ideas, but they were all expressions of *me, me, me*.

Brand values are what the company claims about itself. Importantly, they assume that people care about (or believe in) those values. But a brand storyteller needs to develop experiences that create, convince, or reinforce the notion that those beliefs are important and true. In order to establish a brand value as being important and true, you have to move nonbelievers to become believers in that value.

Put simply: The storyteller needs to establish the *pre-value* existence to build tension and make the audience care about the values in question. In the Nike example, the storyteller needs to bring a world-view that makes acquiring inspiration and innovation a valuable thing for everyone.

Nike does this extraordinarily well in its Dream Crazy ads, giving the audience a satisfying story. The ad features former NFL quarter-back Colin Kaepernick, who went unsigned after becoming a free agent in 2016.[4] Kaepernick voices over examples of famous athletes and regular people who aren't just excelling at their sport but dreaming of making a bigger impact. Many believe that Kaepernick went unsigned because of the controversy surrounding his decision to kneel in protest during the national anthem prior to games and his outspoken nature on civil rights. At the end of the ad, Kaepernick reveals himself as the narrator and says, "Don't ask if your dreams are crazy, ask if they're crazy enough."

Now that's a universal truth we can believe in.

Politics aside, you can immediately see the distinction between Nike's brand story and the brand's story that it told featuring Kaepernick. It was their story (it belongs to them), but it wasn't about them.

Nike celebrates the athlete and supports its brand value with a distinct point of view. (Whether you agree with that point of view or not, the storytellers for that ad are supporting their brand with a tension-filled story.)

On the other hand, when Nike leaned too heavily on its brand value claim of being "proud of its American heritage" and failed to create a compelling narrative to support a shoe with the Betsy Ross version of the American flag, its effort failed.[5] What was missing? The journey was missing—the struggle. They simply tried to equate Betsy Ross, the American flag, and Nike. Half the audience went, "Meh, I don't care," while the other half, of course, did care—but didn't think there was a believable story. So, they made up their own. And, as I just said, it's exceedingly rare that the one that gets created for us works in our favor.

Every great story has what I call a "core truth"—something universal that I want people to believe by telling this story.

The wonderful storytelling coach and messaging strategist Tamsen Webster calls this concept the "red thread" (which I love). When I asked her about it, she explained that the "red thread is the why behind your why." To bring this together with the previous chapter, your "why" is ultimately what your company cares about, and your brand's stories are focused on why your *audience* will care—that's the "why" behind your "why."

Ultimately, it's a subtle but important difference. Your *brand story* says what you want people to believe, and your *brand's stories* must demonstrate *why it's important for the audience to believe it.*

But none of this means that the brand's stories are disconnected from the brand. They are, after all, possessed by the brand.

The story must connect

We have to acknowledge that, for the most part, content marketing practitioners will have minimal or no control over what the over-arching brand stands for. Either changing the brand story is well above your pay grade, or the story has been established for decades, or (and probably most importantly) it's different in the minds of the consumer than it is on your mission statement page.

Content experiences, behavior, and storytelling can help repair the disconnect. But the stories must come from that distinct point of view that helps the brand reclaim something it may have lost.

Most of the time, content marketers can't change the brand (nor do most storytellers have challenges the size of those facing Nike). But they can—and should—aim to support the brand in its mission to establish, bolster, or repair its current claim about itself.

For example, back in 2012, I had the pleasure of interviewing Jonathan Mildenhall, then the Vice President of Advertising Strategy and Creative Excellence at Coca-Cola. Even someone in his lofty position realized the limitations of changing the brand story (no apostrophe) when it came to content.

As we talked about creative excellence in marketing, he said there was no way he could change the brand story. The values weren't going to change. The iconic bottle shape certainly wasn't going to change. The logo wasn't going to change. And the ingredients in the bottle weren't going to change. But Jonathan told me:

> We fully understand that we are still going to have to do promotions,
> price messaging, shopper bundles, traditional ads, etc.—that isn't going

away. But our [brand's stories] are the way consumers understand the role and relevance of the Coca-Cola Company. We have to make sure that those "immediate stories" are part of the larger brand story.[6]

This is why a brand's stories are critical. As storytellers, your role is to understand how to create many original stories that demonstrate why people should care (the why behind the why) about the promise of the overarching brand story.

For example, among LEGO's brand values is that imagination is critical. It says on its website:

Curiosity asks why and imagines explanations or possibilities. Playfulness asks what if and imagines how the ordinary becomes extraordinary, fantasy, or fiction. Dreaming it is a first step towards doing it.[7]

When storytellers create a LEGO brand's story (such as *The LEGO Movie*), they use that foundation like a prism to focus their light on universal truths (or points of view) that show the customer the value of reaching for those universal truths.

Imagine that *The LEGO Movie* was a story about a young, arrogant LEGO hero who is the star builder in a big city. Then, one day he gets lost and finds himself in a small LEGO town where he must learn humility and that friends and family are worth far more than the glory of winning at building.

That's an interesting and fun story—and it also happens to *not* be the story of *The LEGO Movie*. It is, rather, the story of the 2006 Pixar movie *Cars*. But even when you read it, you probably recognized that it didn't sound quite right. It doesn't sound like a LEGO story, does it?

No. Instead, *The LEGO Movie* is about Emmet—an average Joe hero. In fact, Emmet is so "average" that at the beginning of the movie, he really has no personality. He needs a step-by-step instruction book just to get his day going. The movie is about Emmet discovering self-identity, and how dreaming creatively about what *could be* can actually save the world. Now *that* sounds like a LEGO story.

Now that you understand the differences between the brand story and the brand's stories, let's explore a framework for how you can start to build—and, more importantly, pressure-test—the ideas you have for your brand's stories.

Pressure-test for the brand's stories

You've got the beginning of a content marketing product idea. Or you may be trying to repair a content experience that is broken. Whether you're working with your team to establish, bolster, or repair your brand, you may come to an idea for your brand's stories from any number of places. The lightning of an idea may strike in the shower or while walking the dog. Or you might be inspired by an idea that comes out of your team's latest brainstorming stand-up. Or you may inherit a story because your company just acquired a brand that already has a digital magazine or learning platform.

Whatever the genesis for the idea, you may want to pressure-test it to see how deep you can take that story. Perhaps it's a simple performance that's really best served as a surface-level TikTok video or a funny anecdote. Or maybe it's a deeper educational idea that could be explored in a series of webinars or a white paper. Or perhaps it's truly a platform that you can build an entire emotional movie or documentary around.

But how do you know?

Six years ago, my colleague Carla Johnson and I introduced the four archetypes of storytelling in our book *Experiences: The 7th era of marketing*.

I've since been working on modifying that model a bit, and one of the areas where we've seen some interesting progress is in developing a business story structure pyramid.

The story structure pyramid encompasses attributes for each of the four archetypes. The simplest, at the top of the pyramid, is the Performer archetype. The only job of "performer" content is to make you feel something. It might be a joke, a sad poem, or an amazing juggling act. But if you can identify and deliver against the emotional stimulus, you have done your job.

Then, you have the Promoter archetype. This archetype is meant to drive action, or commitment. In order to achieve commitment or action, we need a promise and a point of view. We call this our "new world." Then we need to set up that promise with tension, so we first establish the "old world," and then trigger the question "what if?"

Figure 7.1 The Business Structure Pyramid

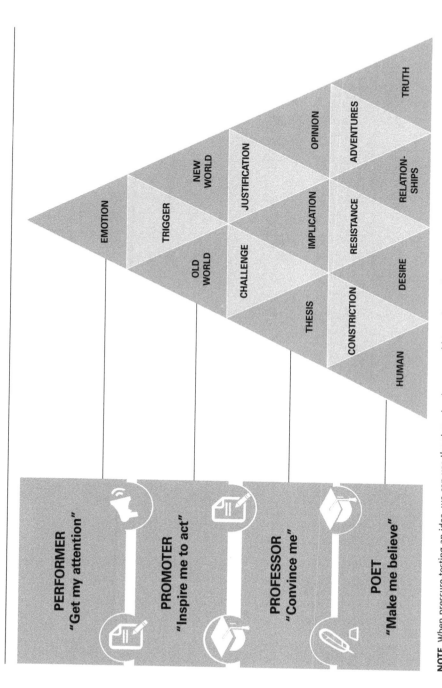

NOTE When pressure-testing an idea, we can use the story structure pyramid to assign attributes to our idea—to ensure we have thought through the best, most well-structured way to develop an idea, based on an idea, on the overall impact we want to have.

Think of those advertisements for knives that you might see on late night television. They usually open with somebody struggling to do the most basic of things, like cutting a potato. "But," the announcer says with anxious excitement, "what if there were a better way?" and then introduces the new cutting tool that slices, dices and does even more than you thought it might. It's a new world for you with this.

The next layer down is the Professor archetype. This category of content is meant to educate or teach you something, and ultimately convince you with an evidence-backed argument. Therefore, it's more complex, and requires a number of attributes that will not only relay the new information to you but do so in a way that makes you trust and believe that you have received accurate, valuable information that you will use. Here, we begin with a thesis (the point of view that we want to teach), but we will also explore any arguments against this thesis, or counter-arguments to our point. We will also provide reasons for our particular point of view on this subject, and why doing it "our way" is better than doing it another way. And we will also provide the implications—both good and bad—about doing it our way, and ultimately get to the valuable lesson that you will receive from this (our POV).

Then, finally, at the other end of the spectrum is the foundation of the pyramid, Poet content. Here there are seven attributes (or pressure points) that are foundational to any complex story, and you must identify and deliver against them to create a satisfying piece of content.

The task is to pressure-test your idea to see if you and/or your team can identify answers for each of the attributes. The more you can identify and describe, the better the chance that your idea has the elements needed to be a great story.

Transforming ideas into story structure: The seven attributes

Developing the "Poet" story is the most challenging, so let's walk through that example. We start by taking the idea that aligns with our audience's job-to-be-done and pressure-testing it against the seven attributes, listed here:

- **The human.** Every great story has a human soul at its core, even if that human is a talking LEGO character or an anthropomorphized cartoon fish. Nobody wants to hear the story of industrial manufacturing. They want to hear the story of Jane, the enigmatic heroine who finds herself challenged with leading a new industrial manufacturer.

- **The constriction.** Good stories have urgency. There is a reason we want to continue past the beginning. A good story sets the early tension and provides a reason for the journey we're about to take. The constriction is something that is pressing our human hero to action. It may be a pulling constriction—something important and perhaps unexpected is demanding action from the human. Or it may be a pushing action—something is pushing them unwillingly into a journey. Either way, the more pressing the better.

- **The goal or desire.** A goal is the conscious or unconscious desire of the human who is pressed into action. The desire to achieve a goal is what continues to propel our human hero through the story journey. When the goal is conscious, it is related to the greater "truth" (as detailed in the final attribute). The superhero team's goal, for example, is simply to defeat the villain. When the goal is unconscious, events transpire in the story that ignite the desire for the illuminated truth in our human hero. Think of a classic detective story, where the hero feels she's getting too old and is pushed to solve the last case so she can retire. However, by solving the most difficult case of her career, the hero also discovers it's the work that keeps her young. The best stories have both conscious and unconscious goals.

- **The resistance(s).** Every great story needs a seemingly insurmountable obstacle. Occasionally, this comes in the form of a great human villain petting a white cat in a secret lair. Other times the resistance is simply a "mountain" that must be climbed or a giant shark that must be killed. The bigger the resistance and the more relatable it is to the hero, the better the story.

- **The relationships.** Your human hero needs relationships with people that represent the best and worst of reaching the goal or desire. There can be any number of these, but they help represent the "lessons learned" or the "assistance" that the human hero needs to achieve the goal. Think Yoda or Obi Wan Kenobi as the mentors to Luke Skywalker. Or the funny sidekick in every romantic comedy you've seen who helps to uncover and solve the hero's self-doubt. Here we want to identify who (or what) can help your human hero achieve the goal. Spoiler alert: In a content marketing sense this may be the person who represents the point of view of your brand in the story.

- **The adventures.** Very much a literal translation, these are the challenges, fights, hills to climb, puzzles to solve, etc. that provide the key progress toward the goal. In the best stories, each adventure gets progressively more difficult, and each represents a metaphoric argument for your truth.

- **The truth.** The truth is your argument—what you believe in and what you are arguing. Some might call this the story's "theme" or "message," but at its core the truth is simply the belief you are trying to inspire in your audience.

So, you take these attributes and ask yourself questions in order to brainstorm your answers and pressure-test the story. How deep should you go? That depends on you, but generally speaking you should be satisfied that the answer is clear:

1 **Who is your human hero?** Identify the person who will be on the journey.

2 **What is the hero's constriction?** What is pressing the hero to action? Something in their world is broken and the hero is being pushed or pulled to fix it.

3 **What is the hero's desire?** What is the conscious or unconscious desire of your human hero?

4 **What is the resistance?** What is the active resistance to your hero? What seems impossible to overcome?

5 What relationships can help? What (or who) are the important relationships that will help your human hero move through this adventure?

6 What are the adventures? What is the series of tests and challenges that must be overcome? Have you truly tested your hero? If you have holes in your story—where your audience will disbelieve your argument—it is usually because you haven't truly tested your hero.

7 What is the truth? What is your argument? It may be connected to a conscious desire, or the hero may discover the truth through the adventures that transpire.

If you answer these questions, you'll have the foundation for a well-structured story. Now, this doesn't mean that your idea is automatically a good one. Even a well-structured story can fail. But you've given yourself a much clearer mission statement for your new content marketing product.

For example, last year I worked with a financial services company on a new content marketing product plan for its digital magazine. The publication wasn't working because the articles came from everywhere in the business and had no consistent value, theme, or point of view. The team wanted a clearly defined—and differentiating—story for the magazine. And, of course, the story needed to match the new brand the company was rolling out.

We started with the four attributes discussed in the previous chapter. We decided that:

A The idea was a whole curriculum and learning platform available digitally.

B The purpose was an "adopt" platform designed to deepen relationships with their existing clients and bolster the idea that the new brand was about helping clients beyond managing portfolios.

C The focuses were client retention/loyalty and an expanded relationship with clients.

D The audience was certified financial advisors with their own firms, who invest through this company on behalf of their clients.

Once we had this content marketing product plan, the question became: What should the story of the curriculum be?

We then worked through the answers to the seven components: hero, constriction, desire, resistance, relationships, adventures, and truth. The team used this information to polish the mission for a new set of classes and thought leadership content targeted toward helping this audience move toward their "so I can" job-to-be-done of "grow my advisory services":

- **The human** hero is today's stressed financial advisor. They are trying as best they can to deliver great services to their clients.

- **The constriction** is the increasing pressure to perform for clients and prove that expertise and money management ability are better than an algorithm delivered by automated trading platforms.

- **The desire** is around these advisors needing and wanting continuing education. They don't need more noise; they need a unique perspective and guidance.

- **The resistance** in the advisor's world is the danger of becoming automated by technology, algorithms, and artificial intelligence. It's an atmosphere that increasingly devalues the human investor and makes trading more like gambling.

- **The relationships** are among expert portfolio managers, trusted colleagues, and genuine industry thought leaders that financial advisors depend on in a network of talent to remain relevant to their clients.

- **The adventures** happen with practice management advice related to news about the economy. We (the financial services company) tackle providing thoughtful answers to everything that today's financial advisor is challenged with.

- **The truth** is that human investing is the only investing. It is a higher calling. New technology should be used, but it should be powered by wisdom. And only human advisors have this ability.

I'm sure you can see how better stories, better posts, and overall differentiation might come from having this framework, rather than "we'll build a news blog for financial advisors."

Further, you probably can start to see how they could (and subsequently did) take the next step and extend the curriculum upward to the professor level, leveraging a thesis, challenge, and implications. Put simply, we can tell the emotional story of the financial advisor *and* we can teach them as well.

Now, to be clear, this is but one kind of story structure that might help. And for any marketing practitioner, I would recommend exploring them all. I've provided a running list of story structure resources on the book's website ContentMarketingStrategy.com.

Now, the most famous story structure is one that you may have heard of, from author and philosopher Joseph Campbell, called "the hero's journey." While all of these story structures are typically lists of elements that, once identified, make your story more likely to be fulfilling, none of them—including mine—should be seen as templates or "fill-in-the-blank" models.

I see the story pyramid in the way Christopher Vogler, author of *The Writer's Journey*, describes Joseph Campbell's hero's journey. I love how Vogler describes the hero's journey as "not an invention, but an observation... a set of principles that govern the conduct of life and the world of storytelling the way physics and chemistry govern the physical world."[8]

In other words, not every great story has an earth-shattering, differentiating answer to every attribute in the story architecture. But the better the answers, the better chance you have something truly worth exploring. The framework can be a tool of expedience, getting to a better story more quickly. Or over a longer time, the framework might help develop a bigger and better brand story where none existed.

I hope this framework becomes another tool in your skill box, helping you to become an amazing brand storyteller in a world that will increasingly value that talent.

Would you like some real-life examples of ideas transformed into business stories, and a full workbook of the story pyramid? It's available at ContentMarketingStrategy.com

Notes

1 McKee, R. (1998) *Story: Substance, structure, style, and the principles of screenwriting*, London: Methuen, p.25

2 Accessed OpenAI.com's ChatGPT on December 15, 2022

3 Nike (2023) Our mission, https://about.nike.com/en (archived at https://perma.cc/AAQ5-2NAZ)

4 AdTV (2018) Nike / Dream Crazy (United States), www.youtube.com/watch?v=WW2yKSt2C_A&t=29s (archived at https://perma.cc/K5Y3-UTJT)

5 CBS Mornings (2019) Nike defends decision to pull Betsy Ross flag shoe, www.youtube.com/watch?v=gghO_mYyczg&t=2s (archived at https://perma.cc/P3FL-4D74)

6 Rose, R. (2012) Content 2020 project brand storytelling lessons, Content Marketing Institute, https://contentmarketinginstitute.com/articles/brand-storytelling-content-2020-3/ (archived at https://perma.cc/S49V-DW3G)

7 LEGO (2018) The LEGO® brand—LEGO Group—about us, www.lego.com/en-us/aboutus/lego-group/the-lego-brand (archived at https://perma.cc/TUE9-KNX9)

8 Vogler, C. (1998) *The Writer's Journey: Mythic structure for storytellers and screenwriters*, London: Pan Books, p.9

Measurement By Design

08

Developing the Right Return on Your Investment

Give me access to your analytics, and I'll have the numbers tell you any story you'd like to hear.

You've heard this before: "What gets measured gets managed."

It's true. But it's also nonsense.

I see so many marketing measurement-focused presentations start with this famous quote—or its corollary, "You can't manage what you can't measure."

Both quotes are typically used to make a case for measuring everything we can. And both are typically attributed either to business strategy guru Peter Drucker or to process expert W. Edwards Deming.

Neither said either phrase. But I'll come back to that.

First, let's just admit something: Measuring marketing is not easy. But why hasn't it ever been made eas*ier*?

In part, because it's arbitrary. Measurement involves determining an incremental value (a size, length, weight, capacity, worth) for something. People have to first agree on a standard of measurement, therefore all measures are based on someone's notion of what the standard should be.

For example, some attribute the definition of a yard to King Henry I of England, who set the measure as the distance between the tip of his nose and the thumb of his outstretched hand. In 1592, England's parliament set the mile at 5,280 feet, or eight furlongs. Since furlongs were 660 feet, we got 5,280 feet in a mile. And how did we get furlongs? They were based on the length of a field an average team of oxen could plow in a day. So, today's mile is based on how much a team of oxen could plow in eight days. Doesn't that make total sense?

However, the more important part of the mile's definition is that we've all agreed on what that measurement means. A standard has been set. Thus, when we say the standard for an automobile's fuel efficiency is "acceptable" at an expenditure of 23 miles per gallon, what we're saying is that we all agree that if a car can travel the distance that an average team of oxen could plow in a little more than six months, using only one gallon of fuel, this qualifies as "good."

That sounds ridiculous on its face. But that's the critical thing to know. Standards (the agreed-upon measurements) by which we all live can only be set by humans when... well, when we arbitrarily set them. An inch isn't an inch because it's an inch. It's an inch because we say it is.

Agreeing is something we humans are only moderately good at. So, it's rare that we all necessarily agree on what the standards are. That doesn't mean we don't try. In fact, in 1799, one of the original measurements of the metric system—the meter—was defined as a "quarter of a 10-millionth of the Earth circumference." That meant they divided the circumference of the world by 10 million, and then quartered that and came up with the standard length of the meter.[1]

But there would be no agreement on that: The metric system, of course, spread as a standard in Europe and other parts of the world but has never been accepted here in the United States.

In 1999, NASA lost a spaceship to this very challenge. The Mars Climate Orbiter was sent to the Red Planet to enter low orbit and study atmospheric changes. Well, as it closed in on Mars, it got too close and was destroyed. This resulted in a $125 million loss. What was the problem? The NASA software system used metric standard units. And the spacecraft builder, Lockheed Martin, used imperial units.[2]

One team based their calculations on how many fields a team of oxen could plow in—let's see, doing my calculations here—one billion three hundred twenty-eight million days (give or take). And another team based their calculations on the distance of 22,500 Earth circumferences (again, give or take). What could possibly go wrong?

Quality vs. quantity makes measurement even more difficult

Okay, so we can probably agree that measuring a simple quantity can be more complex than we thought. How then do we measure quality, where there is, and can be, no set "standard"?

Again, it comes back to agreement.

In his treatise *Metaphysics*, Greek philosopher Aristotle wrestled with how measuring quantities and qualities differs. He said that quantities have equality or inequality, but not degrees. (One person can't be more 5 foot 6 inches than another person.) Qualities, on the other hand, don't have equality or inequality but do have degrees. (Someone can be more or less successful than someone else.) Without getting into the deeply philosophical discussion of "quality," Aristotle concluded that quality was defined by its stability—or its observability in a stable state. Put very simply, we all agree something is the color "blue." But as we, or it, changes, fewer and fewer will agree, until we all agree again that the thing is no longer blue, but another color.

It is the combination of quantitative and qualitative measurement that makes assessing marketing results so darn difficult. Marketing is and always will be both art *and* science. While there are standard definitions for many of the quantitative measures in marketing (click, view, conversion, sale), every single marketing measurement is also a qualitative measurement. There is emotion behind every marketing metric, so the quality (or degree) of the measurement is also critically important. In other words, one view of an ad may be all I need to make a decision about a product or service. But it may take someone else 10 views of the same ad to make a similar decision. Even a "sale" (which seems so simple) can have different degrees of quality. Someone might agree to a sale, only to return (or regret) their purchase after the transaction. Others might purchase with such enthusiasm that they evangelize the transaction to everyone they know. Even though those two sales were monetarily the same, they are hardly equal in value.

The real challenge is that we never get agreement on any of it. Most businesses don't go to the trouble to define their objectives and the measurements that will define progress toward them.

Now, that doesn't mean marketers don't try, or that every agreed-upon standard is a failure. Television offers a great example. At one point, most people agreed that audience attention would be measured by whether the content played on the TV in the observed household. It didn't matter if the people in the house were in rapt attention, arguing, asleep, or not even really watching. There were no degrees of difference. A quantity/quality standard (any "view" is a "good view") was proposed, and enough people agreed on that standard to build a multibillion-dollar industry on it. Nielsen Media Research introduced TV ratings in 1950, and for the last 70 years they have been the "standard" for advertising pricing.

But, of course, because humans are involved in the agreement, all marketing standards change. We change, and so do the things measured. Most, but certainly not all, agreed in 1950 when Nielsen introduced television "ratings" to the world. But as time has progressed, we have arguably reached a point now (in 2023) where both the medium (television) and our agreement on what constitutes "good" (a view) have changed.

What equals a view of a TV audience has been debated, negotiated, and adapted since it began. But as of summer 2022, Nielsen's measurement standards lost their "quality" agreement, and thus the standard is changing. Any number of new technology and measurement companies are trying to become the standard for audience measurement on television. What will ultimately become the standard? We don't know yet. We do know that, like every other marketing measurement, it will assuredly change again.

Every measurement for marketing is also quality measurement. The standards—the goals—are up to us to create. But we must get people to agree to the incremental degrees of improvement we create toward that objective. *Who* clicked? *Why* did they follow us? *How qualified* is the lead? *How much* is too much cost in order to get that sale?

That brings us back to the axiom "what gets measured gets managed." The quote comes from academic V.F. Ridgway, and it is only half of what Ridgway actually said. In 1956, Ridgway was warning about the consequences of businesses reducing everything to meaningless numbers. Here's the complete quote:

> What gets measured gets managed—even when it's pointless to measure and manage it, and even if it harms the purpose of the organization to do so.[3]

Ridgway was warning us to stop measuring everything just because we can. Because, as he said, if you measure it, you are likely to manage it. And guess what? It might not be worth managing.

It's up to us to set the standards for measuring the quality of our success. If you're going to the trouble to get agreement to measure anything, it should be something important—something that defines progress toward a strategic objective.

As I've said to numerous students in my training courses: Don't make things matter because they're measurable. Make them measurable because they matter to you.

Content marketing measurement is different

The activities making up a content marketing strategy are a bit different than those in a traditional marketing organization, as noted throughout the book. That doesn't mean that they aren't aligned, though, and it doesn't mean that they won't resemble some of the classic activities that marketers have performed for years. But they are different.

Let's start with two questions:

What is the overall objective? Where are we focusing our measurement?

What does meeting the objective—success—look like?

Too often in a content marketing approach, the answers to those questions have no relation to each other.

One of my favorite books about data and measurement is *The Haystack Syndrome* by Eli Goldratt. It's almost 30 years old, but it's more relevant than ever. In the book, Goldratt proposes a method to architect a system to appreciate the difference between data and information (hint: One has context and thus impacts action) and achieve a true business measurement.

A quote from the book may resonate with any of you who have struggled to find relevant measurement in content marketing for your business:

> Tell me how you will measure me and I will tell you how I will behave. If you measure me in an illogical way, don't complain about illogical behavior.[4]

When my consulting firm works with a company to evolve its measurement strategy for content marketing, two primary challenges appear. First, the company usually has no agreed-upon, specific purpose or goal for its content marketing initiative. It's usually some amorphous version of *"just make our regular marketing stuff better."* Thus, many businesses simply define their content marketing as an ability to produce ad hoc digital content assets that supplement their "normal marketing," and they measure performance as they would any other marketing campaign-focused asset.

This is the first mistake: only measuring the *content performance quantity*, not the *quality of the impact* that the content has on the audience (see where this is going?).

The result of measuring only content transactions is that the content marketing team is then stuck using (or resolved to use) vanity metrics on the content itself, such as clicks, shares, visits, etc. It's interesting to know that the blog post or infographic was found and read, but what behavior did it change? We don't know, because we're only measuring the quantifiable actions taken on the content and have no agreement on what those quantifiable actions even mean.

That gets us to the second challenge. Many businesses don't understand how to connect that impact on audience to an optimized behavior (meaning one we like) other than as a sale of our product or service. In other words, it's neat that we have 5,000 people in our content marketing email list, but the only behavioral impact we understand (or value) is that they *might* become sales transactions. So, the only question becomes "*When are we going to convert them into leads, or sales?*" Content marketers then push back: If we try to sell to them now, won't that alienate them? The answer is, you don't know.

Okay, wait a minute. If content can convert audiences into sold customers, shouldn't marketers be able to track that?

Maybe. Maybe not. We haven't agreed on anything yet.

Shouldn't we just measure everything, whether we understand it or not, so that we can see what happens?

Funnily enough, the second half of Eli Goldratt's wonderful quote answers that nicely:

> ... if you change my measurements to new ones, that I don't fully comprehend, nobody knows how I will behave, not even me.

It doesn't matter whether you don't understand the objectives or you don't know how to associate content consumption metrics to the goals you *do* understand. The fact is, you don't fully comprehend what it is you're trying to do. Therefore, no one really understands why you're doing it. Not even you.

So, in a content marketing strategy, you have to begin by acknowledging that content marketing measurement is different than marketing measurement, even though it shares many of the same properties. You must understand—and be sure others understand—that the value you will create lies in the qualitative behavior change of the audience, not the content itself.

Let's come back to our two questions and take them one by one.

What is our overall business objective?

Chapter 5 discussed the possibility that a business can view its relationship with audiences as it does its relationship with customers. It asked what could happen if you viewed your ability to reach them as an "audience asset" that actually increases in value over time.

The conclusion was that you wouldn't simply measure the size of the audience; you would measure how much the audience (specifically the different kinds of audience members) added wealth to your business. You would measure both the quantity *and* quality of that audience.

So, if the reason that we set up a content marketing strategy is so that we might put a tangible financial value on the depth and dimension of the behavior of that audience (in other words, subscribed audiences do stuff that others don't and help you create more value), then it makes sense to define business objectives that align with that financial value.

Let's start with the highest-level strategic objectives for your business. As it turns out, there are really only two kinds of activities valued by businesses: The first is if the activity helps to generate more revenue, and the second is if it helps save on costs. You may argue that there are others, such as contribute to the environment, or improve society in some way (and I wouldn't necessarily disagree with you). But if either of those first two are not met, the business can't really make meaningful progress to others.

Then, the way we perform these activities can directly or indirectly affect these two objectives. For example, creating a paid customer education event like Salesforce's Dreamforce event might be a natural extension to other, more traditional, products and services (while also expanding our brand's relationship). This content program is then a *direct* contributor to more revenue, while it also serves a marketing purpose. However, creating an online, unpaid, customer loyalty community creates greater retention for existing customers, and therefore only influences how long a customer stays loyal to a brand. It is then an *indirect* contribution to more revenue.

If we put this together, we end up with four categories of strategic objectives. How can a content marketing strategy help us achieve:

- **Indirect savings:** helping us with insight that aids our ability to make other activities more efficient.
- **Direct savings:** contributing directly to a more efficient marketing engine, at less cost than other methods.
- **Indirect revenue:** influencing the customer to spend more, subscribe longer, or in some way purchase more from our company.
- **Direct revenue:** driving revenue for the company.

Figure 8.1   Direct and Indirect Measurement of Content Marketing

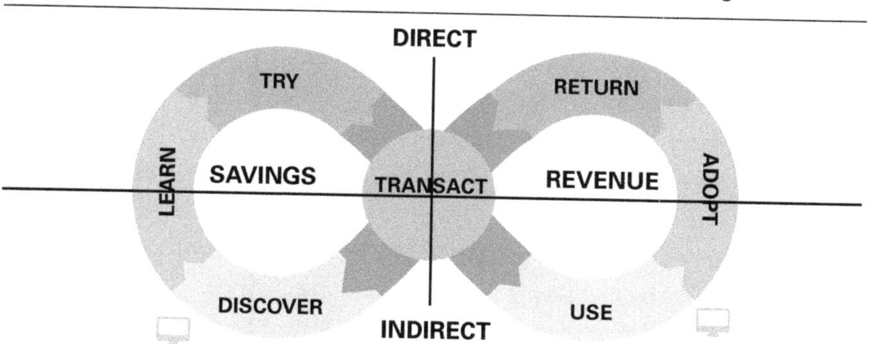

NOTE Marketers can generally align their content marketing goals across the customer's journey against indirect and direct savings and revenue objectives.

With those categories in mind, let's return to the infinity loop customer journey. Generally speaking (and there are exceptions to be sure), if you look at your customer's journey and then plot the four resulting categories of revenue and savings, you'll end up with a graph that looks a bit like the one here.

You'll remember the lower left is the early part of the customer's journey—discovery and brand awareness. This is where content marketing activities are primarily focused on indirect savings. In other words, this is where we focus on branding/awareness efforts and gaining wider reach, and how content marketing can help us make our company smarter, or get that reach more efficiently.

As an example, a content platform that helps the business optimize its placement in search rankings will help drive more high-level traffic to the company's website. This more organic (or inexpensive) effort equates to more "free" awareness, thus indirectly making it less expensive for the business to generate interest in its products or services.

Then, the upper left shows the middle to end of the buying journey, where "buyer" becomes "customer." The activities here are primarily about direct savings, or efficiency. This is where you apply the ROI formula we discussed in Chapter 5. You look at how efficiently you can create a new customer. So, content marketing in this part of the customer's journey is directly contributing to more leads, better leads, or an acceleration of their journey toward customer. There is a direct savings to marketing expenses calculation (or a multiplier effect, as the case may be) as a focus of measurement.

In the lower right-hand quadrant is the post-sale experience that marketing may have some responsibility for. These are upgrade marketing programs, loyalty efforts, or other marketing activities that may indirectly generate additional revenue. These programs influence the customer's relationship with your brand and how the customer is getting the best and most valuable use of your product or service. So, for example, your content marketing program may be focused on helping the customer understand all the accessories they may want to get the most out of their product, or on educating the customer on how the product can be optimally utilized. So the measurement is your ability to influence a reduction in returns, or increased length of subscription, or upsell opportunities for additional products.

Finally, in the upper right quadrant are the return or extension programs that transform existing customers into higher-value customers, or extend other types of marketing assets (such as intellectual property, events, or other valuable content) into direct revenue. Activities here include revenue-generating customer loyalty events, or even the licensing of marketing-oriented intellectual property (IP) to other brands. This is where content marketing programs themselves can become direct revenue opportunities.

For example, in my book *Killing Marketing*, with my colleague Joe Pulizzi, we spoke with Sangram Vajre, co-founder and chief marketing officer at Terminus, a software company focused on account-based marketing. We wrote about how Vajre built a content marketing brand called "Flip My Funnel," which was an idea that the company began to package into all of their various channels (blog, social media, etc.). Then, as Vajre put it in our book:

> We put an event together in a couple of months and invited all top leaders in the marketplace that cared about the topic. Nothing to do with Terminus... not a single person spoke at the conference about Terminus. Ten sponsors [helped] to pay for the conference... It was almost like... no real money spent [was] from us because it was all

taken care of by the sponsorship(s). We were able to bring in 300 to 400 people to attend the conference... and we were able to build relationships with all these top leaders.[5]

Terminus's Flip My Funnel "Revenue Summit" became an instant success. After the first event, Terminus was able to close 15 significant customers directly from the event. Terminus then went on to launch events in cities around the country.

What the Terminus story also illustrates is that, as you expand your content marketing ideas to other parts of the journey, you may also start to measure it in multiple ways. You can see how Terminus started their efforts by creating a marketing event that paid for itself. However, its success then evolved their opportunity to also measure it as a lead generation engine, and a loyalty program for their existing customers.

Ultimately, these four quadrants are not designed to lock you into a measurement box for your efforts; they are to help you focus your initial efforts. One of the most difficult things to do when launching a content marketing strategy is focus where we will measure. Because content marketing takes a significant amount of effort, our immediate desire is to measure everything we possibly can. However, we learned in Chapter 5 that we want to initially focus our efforts on one audience. And we learned in Chapter 6 that we want to begin our focus on one part of the journey. So, it makes sense that we would start setting our goals and objectives with that same idea. So, pick one overall business objective to start, and focus your key goals and objectives in that quadrant.

That gets us to the second question that starts us on designing a measurement program.

What does success look like?

Now you have an overall focus for beginning your measurement plan. You know you want to measure the impact you are having on the audiences you reach with your content marketing initiatives. And you also know that whether you initially focus on indirect or direct savings, or revenue, depends on where the focus of your content marketing is in the customer's journey.

Figure 8.2   Direct and Indirect Measurement With the 5Cs

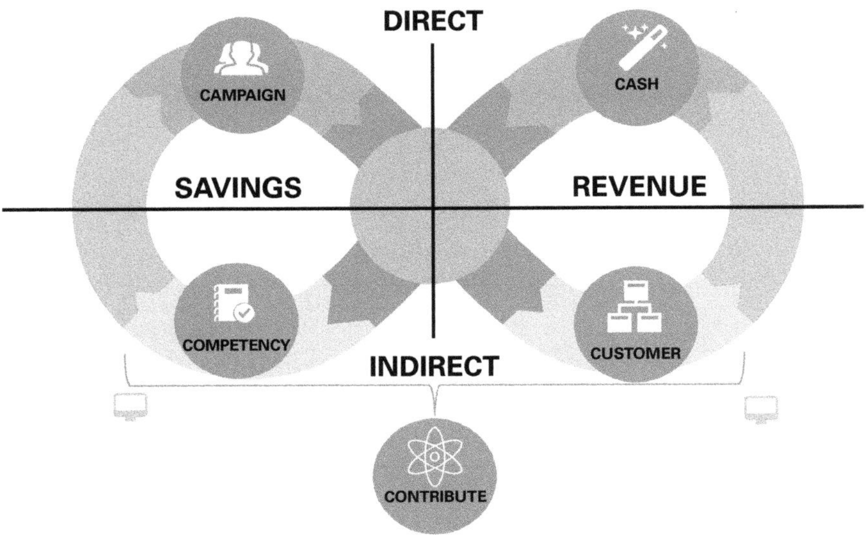

NOTE Each category (except one) of what success looks like aligns with the customer's journey and indirect and direct savings and revenue. The fifth—Contribution—applies to the whole of the journey.

The next step is to address the question of (and get agreement on) "What does success look like?"

One useful way to break down the answers to that question is to explore the possible categories of focus that align with the business objective that we just set. We call these the 5 Cs of Audience Investment Value. They are:

1 Contribution

2 Competency

3 Campaign

4 Customer

5 Cash

Though each C can be broken into subcategories with different types of objectives appropriate for different kinds of companies, each one (except for one) also generally aligns with the customer's journey as well. You can see how this overlays our direct and indirect model from earlier.

Contribution value

This is the one exception, as it extends across the entirety of the customer's journey and is focused almost exclusively on efficiency (or savings). As we discussed in Chapter 3, one of the ways that a content marketing strategy can begin is within the Producer model, where there is an internal "agency" that is charged with supplying content marketing assets to either one or multiple departments within a business. In this case, the team's measurement may only be an internal metric of how effectively that agency can perform against the needs of the broader business. Here we will not be measuring audiences as much as we are the overall contribution of content marketing to the efficiency of any of the other marketing and communications across the customer journey. For example, we may measure overall cost, or quantity of content that is consumed by the internal groups. Or we may measure quality of content against search engine optimization, or social media distribution, by the source (e.g., author) of the content.

With an overall goal of "savings" (either direct or indirect) the focus here is on how the content team *contributes* to the overall health of the marketing and sales program.

Competency value

Once we begin looking at a subscribed audience, however, we can start to focus in on success as to how that audience asset enables smarter, more cost-effective business strategies. Investing in a subscribed audience is not just about aggregating enough data on people to optimize the timing of sales or other offers. Remember, subscribers provide data willingly and trustingly. Thus, it is more valuable than data gleaned from third parties or acquired via purchase. This value exchange means that the data (or productive usage of the data—the insight) you gather can add wealth to your business. Audience insights from the appropriate usage of the *right* data can make your business much smarter about what products you offer, where you offer them, and how you position them. Audience data can help by providing contextual information to make your digital experiences personalized, or more targeted.

For example, Schneider Electric, a global company specializing in energy management and automation solutions with more than $25 billion in revenue, has a multitude of marketing and sales efforts across the world. One of them, sitting squarely in the "brand-building" part of the customer's journey, is an audience-building platform called Energy University, a free e-learning resource for engineers.

This content product delivers courses in 12 languages and has been endorsed by more than a dozen professional and trade organizations for continuing education credits. Over the last few years more than 180,000 learners have gone through the university.

One of the biggest benefits Schneider receives from this platform is the ability to use the students' data to understand them better and learn what products they may ultimately be looking to buy. This insight is incredibly valuable to product marketers and executives as they look to highlight or introduce new product lines.

If you can begin to gather more valuable data from your audience, you can become a more competent company and you'll start to provide indirect savings to many other parts of the business trying to do other things.

Campaign value

Audiences enable traditional marketing and advertising to be more efficient.

Remember, in classic marketing and advertising the main effort to reach audiences is to spend money on campaigns that attempt to optimize how many of the right eyeballs can be reached. And then, the goal is to measure the ratio of that cost to the number of those people who do what the campaign wanted them to do.

One of the earliest measurable goals of content marketing and audience engagement is to make these campaigns more efficient or effective. In my friend Joe Pulizzi's book *Epic Content Marketing*, he writes about Indium, a company that refines, produces, supplies, and fabricates indium chemicals for the electronics semiconductor, solar, thin-film, and thermal management markets:

> Seventeen engineers from materials supplier Indium have discovered content gold with their From One Engineer to Another blog. Through it, they produce valuable content, videos, and answer questions about

a variety of engineering topics (for example, how to set up and operate the Indium sulfamate plating bath).[6]

According to Indium's marketing director, leads jumped 600 percent after the blog's launch. If we then compare the classic "spend of advertising reach" vs. "cost of the blog," we can see that, for Indium, the leads generated from the blog are much less expensive than the traditional marketing they are doing. Success, in this case, looks like a less expensive way to generate better leads than traditional advertising.

Customer value

Audiences give us the opportunity to create better customers.

One of the best ways to measure what audiences do, that others don't, is to see if they buy more initially upon or shortly after becoming a customer. Can you teach your customers to be better customers?

Customer events, content-driven apps, and even print magazines are used not only to make customers feel better about their purchase, but also to provide separate, discrete value from the brand.

Consider Nike. The company began developing branded apps back in 2006. Now it has multiple mobile apps focused on helping runners and athletes track their progress. As *Ad Age* reported, collectively, these apps boast a user base of over 28 million people.[7] That is 28 million people the brand has direct access to—subscribers, if you will. With this greater customer intimacy, Nike gains invaluable insights and information about its customer base. The company could have used its access to all this information to aggressively drive sales from the apps, but instead Nike brilliantly created an authentic athlete community by means of its apps and indirectly drives revenue through greater loyalty.

That is the power of an aggregated audience, and it changes the remit of marketing considerably.

Cash value

As we've discussed a few times in this book, one of the biggest benefits of a content marketing strategy is the opportunity to generate revenue from marketing activities.

Joe Pulizzi and I wrote an entire book on this category and how it is changing marketing from a cost center into the possibility of being a profit center for business. In our book *Killing Marketing*, we demonstrate that marketing with content can also be a business model. Leading companies are diversifying their businesses, generating higher margins, and/or mitigating costs of other marketing activities. They are, when combined with the savings attributed to other values, marketing at a profit.

As mentioned earlier, one of the best representations of this is Salesforce and its Dreamforce event. The event charges money for attendees, and for sponsors to have a booth at the event. At an average registration fee of $1,600, that is $64 million in revenue without accounting for additional event-related revenue such as corporate sponsorships and/or other licensing.

Consider that the average market valuation of trade show events for media companies is three to five times revenue; that means that if you were to break out Salesforce's Dreamforce content marketing platform as a separate company, it would have current revenues (tickets and sponsorships) just shy of $100 million and be worth somewhere between $200 million and half a billion dollars. That means Dreamforce is not just a marketing program, it is truly an asset to the business. It is not only driving top-line revenue, but is a key component of shareholder value for Salesforce.

The key to understanding these 5 Cs of value is that marketers agree that these objectives are worth pursuing. Remember, we're not yet at "analytics." We've only answered the first two questions of what our overall objective is, and what success looks like. There is no "dashboard" (yet) to see the value of our answers. You not only have to agree that the objective is worth pursuing, but also agree on the unambiguous measurement that will define progress toward that focused objective.

Once you define the qualitative degrees of "value" in these objectives, you need to design the quantitative measures of what will signify progress toward them. You roll up your sleeves, run tests, design measurement programs, and hypothesize targeted indicators that will help you agree on the productivity of your efforts. For example, you might decide to do any of the following:

- Retrieve a segment of a subscribed audience for a targeted advertising campaign to test whether previous engagement helps provide less expensive reach or higher conversions. This would be testing what success looks like for Campaign-focused value.

- Poll and survey your audience members to understand them more deeply and learn how you might deliver better sales offers to them that convert at a higher rate. This would be establishing better insight for value for a Competency-focused objective.

- Personalize your website using data obtained during their subscription to your newsletter and use data to serve more optimized e-commerce catalog products to see if it lifts shopping cart value. You could even do this post-purchase as a follow-up. This is testing a Campaign-focused value that perhaps crosses over into Customer value.

- Tag audiences as they work through the buyer's journey, and partner with sales to deliver insight as to what the customer is interested in, so sales can have more relevant conversations with buyers and see if these content marketing leads close at a higher rate. This is a Campaign-oriented value that helps sales close more business.

- Measure organic vs. purchased traffic to see if audiences are acquired more efficiently or effectively, and/or if they are more likely to turn into leads over time. This is a Competency-focused effort that helps you determine how to be more efficient with your ad dollars.

In short, successful content marketers measure their efforts by using the value of the audience asset and applying the observed impact of content as a tool to garner value to the business. Put simply, we answer the question, "What do subscribed audiences do (or help us do) that others do not?"

This provides value that can grow in two ways. The audience can grow in size (thus increasing the impact of any one measurement). And it can grow in quality and diversity (thus increasing the number of success goals it might support).

The critical thing, as Eli Goldratt might say, is to first understand what success looks like. You should have hypotheses you can test. So when someone asks, "What does success look like?," you have a clear and distinct answer. Then, when asked, "What are you trying to measure?," you can specify exactly what is needed to understand your progress toward that success.

Now you know how you will behave. It's logical. How do you measure content marketing? You don't measure the content. You continuously measure your audience's "health" on the business-given specific objectives.

But how do you come up with those quantitative measurements? How do you transform those business goals into an analytics plan?

Designing the content marketing strategy measurement

Welcome to the wonderful world of quantitative content marketing analytics.

It's at this point where I hear you saying, "I was told there would be no math in marketing." The good news is that all kinds of tools will help you do all that math.

The bad news is that none of these tools will help you understand what the numbers mean for your business.

As we've said, shared objectives without analytics are visions without a map. And deciding on analytics without objectives is like having a map but nowhere to go.

If you have a shared objective and a common understanding of how you'll know if you've met it, only then can you define it with numbers. That's when the numbers have a purpose, and, more importantly, meaning.

Think of your company as a team with the shared goal of winning the game. Everyone on the team knows you need to score more points than your opponent to win. But without a common understanding of how many points result from a field goal or a touchdown, you won't know if you've scored enough points until someone's declared the winner. If you end up losing, it's too late to fix anything. If you somehow win, nobody understands why.

Your goal is to architect your shared objectives with crystal-clear, unambiguous measurements of success. You want to establish this architected measurement so that everyone across the company agrees.

This isn't about everybody getting to define their own standards (à la Lockheed and NASA agreeing among themselves on metric vs. imperial). Your designed measurement plan must be communicated, shared, and expressly agreed upon by everyone.

As a vice president of marketing once said to me:

> The sales team is measured on the value of the opportunities that turn into customers. Marketing is measured by the number of leads created. That sounds like a match—but it's not. We create a huge number of leads looking for introductory products, but the sales team only cares about the leads we create for enterprise products. We're both meeting our objectives, but we're losing for the business.

If you don't have a clearly defined (and shared) vision for what success looks like, you can't measure anything meaningful in content marketing or any other department.

One useful measurement architecture that emerged in the last decade is a concept called objectives and key results (OKRs). OKRs are a fantastic method for getting to the measurement that matters. They help ensure progress toward a shared destination.

A great way to think of OKRs is to just fill in the blanks in this statement:

> We will [your objective] as measured by [key results]

For our purposes, we've modified this methodology slightly for content marketing strategy. We call this the content marketing Measurement Pyramid.

The pyramid is a framework that you can utilize to assign a shareable objective and understand the important (and well-understood) meaning of progress toward that objective. There are four levels to each pyramid:

A The Objective. A shared and well-understood goal. Objectives should align to the charter and responsibilities identified in Chapter 3, and are the result of understanding the overall business goal, and what success looks like.

B The Key Results. The unambiguous investment values that will

Figure 8.3 The Measurement Pyramid

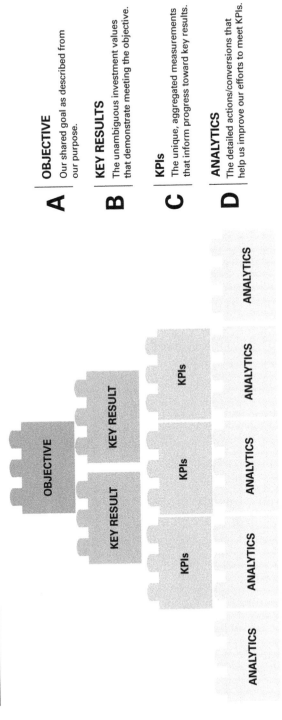

A | **OBJECTIVE**
Our shared goal as described from our purpose.

B | **KEY RESULTS**
The unambiguous investment values that demonstrate meeting the objective.

C | **KPIs**
The unique, aggregated measurements that inform progress toward key results.

D | **ANALYTICS**
The detailed actions/conversions that help us improve our efforts to meet KPIs.

NOTE There are four levels to account for in order to design a measurement approach that everyone can agree on.

demonstrate we have met the objective. This is a combination of factors that you all agree accurately describes "what success looks like."

C The KPIs (Key Performance Indicators). The unique aggregated measurements that inform progress toward the key results.

D The Analytics. The detailed transactional conversions, conversations, and other single data points that make up the measurement of the KPIs.

With this framework in mind, you can build one measurement pyramid for each of your strategic objectives.

Here is the process.

Step 1: Set the objective

Ensure you create an actual and shareable objective. Well-articulated strategic objectives capture a mix of how content will deliver value to the business. They also imply or overtly talk about a time horizon—when the success will happen.

Now, you may plan to realize objectives (or not) by the quarter, year, or multiple years. You might have long-term and short-term objectives. You can figure out the hierarchy of those things.

Setting strategic objectives doesn't mean they don't change as the marketplace shifts or assumptions evolve. It just means you can start to time-box them to understand how quickly you need to change.

For example, pretend your business agrees that the strategic objective is to ensure your new thought leadership blog is a valuable platform for the business. Your overall objective then is: Our blog will be a profitable source of new leads for our marketing.

You can see this objective belongs in the upper left part of the journey as discussed previously (direct savings) and is squarely in the Campaign category of value. You can also see in the objective that it's not just a source of new leads at any cost. Your blog is designed to be a *profitable source of new leads*.

Now that you have a shareable strategic objective, move to the next step.

Step 2: Define success with the key results

Decide the key results that will unambiguously define accomplishing that objective.

The shareable objective for the content marketing team is to become a profitable source of new leads. But what is the definition of that? How many leads? What does profitable mean?

So, the next step is to define the key results that the business will agree are standards that define the objective. So, perhaps you agree on these key results:

- The blog produces 10 percent of all net new sales qualified leads within one year.
- The blog produces 2,000 total addressable subscribers within one year.
- The leads produced by the blog are 10 percent less expensive than standard lead acquisition.
- Organic traffic to the blog represents 20 percent of your total website traffic.

There could be others here, but the idea is that you identify a handful (not dozens) of key results that will define what a profitable source of leads means. The reason to have more than one KPI, but not too many, is that there are degrees of achieving KPIs that need to be determined for defining success. For example, we may meet three of the four key results (perhaps we achieve only 9.5 percent of all net new sales and we must determine if that then becomes a pass or fail for the objective). You won't be surprised to learn that my advice for determining this is that you simply get agreement for each one.

You have a shared objective and you've defined how the impact on the audience will have a direct effect on profit over cost. That gets you to Step 3.

Step 3: Design your KPIs

As I mentioned, one of the challenges of your key results is that each one is probably better defined as a combination of measurements than one single measurement. For example, the key result that "blog leads will be 10 percent cheaper than standard leads" can be reached in a number of ways. You might find that people who subscribe to your blog are actually more expensive to acquire than high-level leads for a "free trial." However, you may also find that blog subscribers convert into qualified leads at a much higher rate than those who sign up for a "free trial." Therefore, these combinations of metrics actually determine the true "expense" of the lead.

Designed KPIs help you get to the best definitions of how to measure progress toward reaching your key results. So, for example, there may be quite a few KPIs that will help you better determine your progress. In this example, we might look at the following KPIs:

- Subscriber counts
- Subscriber vs. visitor and lead form fills
- Conversion rates by content promotion methods (paid vs. organic)
- A-level (sweet spot) subscribers vs. B-level subscribers such as competitors, students, etc.
- Paid traffic vs. organic traffic levels, and cost

You get the idea. This is the equivalent of help with understanding the in-game analytics data to help you play a better game. You know the objective, and you know what success looks like, now you just have to see the multiple ways of getting there and how they all play nicely with each other. You may discover, for example, that it's easy to develop high-quality leads, but that the cost is higher than traditional marketing. Locking yourself into only one way of looking at things limits your ability to make a business decision about what is acceptable for now.

This is the whole idea of KPIs—they *indicate* performance. They help us make adjustments to everything, including our overall results or even the objective.

That leads to the final step.

Step 4: Assemble your analytics

Once you understand the KPIs, you need to begin to identify the specific analytics—the granular measurements that will define the continuous health of your individual KPIs.

Analytics tools are just as they are defined—they are built to measure the granular, transactional elements of "what happens." They are not built to measure "why" it happens. It is up to us to examine our KPIs and then assemble the precise analytics we will utilize to define the measurement of improvements or progress toward them.

For example, with perhaps dozens of KPIs associated with the example here, you can then look to the various metrics that will help you understand how your actions are impacting progress toward them. You might look at:

- Likes and follows on social media that promotes our blog
- Shares of content from our blog
- Traffic, time on site, bounce rates
- Cost of content production
- Cost of the traffic being generated
- SEO rankings for specific keywords

Again, you get the idea.

That sounds like a lot of work. Spoiler alert: It is. Nobody said this was going to be easy. And guess what? You need to do this for all of your objectives.

Measurement is more than just math

So, what does this look like when it's all designed? It looks like a lot of pyramids. You see the overall business mission segmented into a few strategic objectives. Each objective connects to a content marketing Strategy Pyramid and source tools for each metric that goes into it.

Ultimately, success in content marketing—actually, all marketing full stop—cannot be mathematically proven. So, in a universe where marketing can never be mathematically proven, what good is math?

Well, as it turns out, it's immensely valuable. It just needs one thing: a shared sense of what success looks like.

In business, what's always true is that if we don't know why we're measuring something, we'll always settle for less of what we want. And if we don't all have a shared idea of what we want, we can be sure we'll never find it.

It bears repeating: Shared objectives without analytics are visions without a map. And analytics without objectives are like a map with nowhere to go.

If we start with a shared objective, and we have a common understanding of what meeting it looks like, then we can define it with math. That's when the numbers have a purpose and, more importantly, meaning.

And that's when we all know we're winning a game that's actually fun to play.

In addition to a sample measurement plan, we have a measurement workbook that can help you answer the right questions and develop your own personal measurement strategy. It's available at ContentMarketingStrategy.com

---

Notes

1 Wikipedia Contributors (2023) Metre convention, https://en.wikipedia. org/wiki/Metre_Convention (archived at https://perma.cc/BWC5-GXJG)

2 Sawyer, C. (1999) Mystery of Orbiter crash solved, *Washington Post*, www.washingtonpost.com/wp-srv/national/longterm/space/stories/ orbiter100199.htm (archived at https://perma.cc/A9FL-2NFN)

3 Ridgway, V.F. (1956) Dysfunctional consequences of performance measurements, *Administrative Science Quarterly*, 1(2), p.240, doi:https:// doi.org/10.2307/2390989 (archived at https://perma.cc/2TQS-URCK)

4 Goldratt, E.M. (1990) *The Haystack Syndrome*, North River Press, Great Barrington, MA, p.35

5 Pulizzi, J. and Rose, R. (2018) *Killing Marketing: How innovative businesses are turning marketing cost into profit*, New York: McGraw-Hill Education, p.78

6 Pulizzi, J. (2014) *Epic Content Marketing: How to tell a different story, break through the clutter, and win more customers by marketing less*, New York: McGraw-Hill Education, p.300

7 Natanson, E. (2016) Best practices: How to use apps to drive loyalty and revenue, *Ad Age*, https://adage.com/article/digitalnext/practices-apps-drive-loyalty-revenue/305398 (archived at https://perma.cc/5PJY-GKEC)

Story Mapping   09
Writing the Road Map to Your Content Marketing Strategy

A content marketing strategy can't get big without learning what it means to be big.

We've talked about quite a bit in the eight preceding chapters. How are you ever going to pull all this together?

Any one of these chapters may be your focus right now. You may be part of a fully functioning marketing team and you just need to get sharper on the stories you're telling. I hope Chapter 7 gives you a focused process for getting there. Or perhaps you need to know your audiences better. I hope Chapter 5 gives you the business case and approach you need to go do that research.

You may be a new marketer looking to take a startup company to great heights over the next year. I hope you don't believe that the first few chapters aren't for you. Even if you are a team of one, defining your purpose and where you will devote your time is incredibly important. It's not uncommon to see a content marketing team of one person. But they create a charter and a focus for their position. They set up a process where they plan and prioritize content with an editorial board (just them and their immediate supervisor over a sandwich). And they ultimately focus on being a product manager for the company blog, driving better reach to their target market and driving more visitors to the company website. The important thing is what you prioritize, and how you make this useful for you.

One of the most common questions I get from small teams is: "How do we make the time for content marketing?" Well, I hate to break it to you, but none of us is afforded any more time in a day than anyone else. So, what you're really asking is: "How do I prioritize content marketing given all my other tasks?" Your knee-jerk reaction may be to outsource it to an agency or freelancer, which is a common thought when considering something new and innovative. I would encourage you to do the opposite. I would suggest that the way you make room for a content marketing strategy is to outsource all those things you already know how to do (because that's easiest to supervise) and then develop your capacity to do the new, innovative practice of content marketing. But, in order to do that, you need to document and be aware of your purpose and your charter—as well as all the things that need to be done that you'll transfer to the out-sourced partner.

See how that all works?

Finally, maybe you're a student looking to see what's really going on in business rather than what you've been taught at university. Some of the things in the earlier chapters may have surprised you. Hopefully, as you enter the job market, many of these frameworks can become new, differentiated skills that you'll bring to a new job.

In all cases, as I said at the beginning of the book, bringing these eight chapters to bear is a new and different world for most businesses. You're walking a tightrope.

Do you know which part of a tightrope walk takes the most courage?

Most people believe it's the first step out on the rope. But the tight-rope walker who narrates one of the short stories in the collection *Vigilantes of Love* says that's not the case:

> The hardest was the step after the first. That's where you gained or lost your balance. That's where it becomes a walk or a fall. After the second step, there is no going back.[1]

The same holds when developing an innovative content marketing strategy—the second step is the hardest.

There are no templates

In the fall of 2022, I was coaching the vice president of content operations at a technology company. She'd recently gotten the mandate to build an innovative content strategy and a new team. But she wasn't sure how to start.

"I've spent so much time at conferences and workshops," she told me. "I've read successful case studies and thought, 'I can do that too.' But now that I have the OK to start, I want to find the best map to follow."

The desire to find a content marketing strategy map, template, or guide hits nearly everyone starting a new initiative like this. But I've found that developing new content strategies by copying someone else's lens rarely produces impressive results.

I've noticed that when people ask, "Can we do what they did?," they usually come up with one of these three answers:

1 If they did that, we surely can

You may have felt this way after reading about some of the examples in this book. This response often comes with a hint of jealousy. It dismisses the person or team but weirdly applauds the map they created. For example, in 2021, an NFT (non-fungible token) sold for $69 million. It was created by computer scientist-turned-artist Beeple. Many people who heard about the sale thought, "Wow, an overpriced JPEG? I could do that!"

But here's the thing. They didn't. Beeple did—and got paid for it. That's the lesson. One of the most important things to realize about Cleveland Clinic's extraordinary success in content marketing is that Amanda Todorovich grew into that position. She didn't start the program; she inherited it by being promoted into the leadership position. It was her vision to continue, enhance, and change the program that evolved it to where it is today.

2 Give me the map to their program, and I'll be as successful

This response, which I call the template process, comes up often in marketing. People look for the prototypical case study, the template, or "proven" best practices to follow. They want the "checklist." And they expect to get the same results.

I've rarely seen teams following this approach end up with the results promised by that original template or fascinating case study. The map is never exactly right for where they're going.

Why? Because it doesn't allow for their particular skills or unique context.

You have to customize a template or map to suit your circumstance. Think of meals you've prepared for friends and family. How often do you change the recipe to suit what you have on hand, what's in season, or what appeals to the people you're making it for?

3 Does anything like what I want to do already exist?
This is the most helpful response, because it involves looking for guidance in content projects or strategies that reflect the *essence* of what you want to achieve. This is where the frameworks of this book will be most helpful for you.

You may find it useful to look outside your industry or even at the most dissimilar and study the essence of what made those efforts successful. Looking beyond the familiar pushes you to interpret the idea through your creative lens.

Instead of duplicating the exact form of the projects you study, look for them to spark your own innovation.

My client at the technology company benefited from this approach as she considered the challenges of leading new people, creating new workflows, and producing new outputs to support a new content marketing strategy.

I advised her to look for projects involving a disruptive change at a company that's nothing like where she works. She ended up studying how a colleague of mine had implemented an internal product design team for a financial services company.

The details differed, yet the example inspired her to discover new approaches she could bring to her process.

Why the first step isn't the doozy

This kind of answer to the question "Can we do that?" reveals why the second step becomes the most difficult.

Think about it. Discovering the spark of innovation offers direction. You've found a lighthouse to sail toward.

But that second step involves committing to a vision. That's when you walk or fall. That's when there's no going back—and there's no one to pin the decision on but yourself.

I helped my client prepare to take the steps she needed to make the changes her new content strategy required.

Whether you're looking to apply one or more of the frameworks in this book to your own business, or you're going to try and do the entire thing from scratch, I hope you'll get value out of the following technique I worked on with my client.

Make your own story map

The term story mapping is used in a number of past and current contexts. It is most predominant as a component of Agile software development, where it refers to the idea of grouping user "behaviors" (or stories) as a workflow to describe how software should behave.

This is, in turn, a byproduct of the Extreme Programming movement of the late 1990s, which employed user stories (or use cases) as a way to develop products.

Today, the practice of story mapping in software development enables architects to arrange the user "stories" into models that help them understand how the broader functionality of a larger software product should be developed. It helps establish a context for the developers to identify gaps or omissions in the development, and more effectively plan and map larger releases or versions of the product.

Additionally, story mapping is a term used by those in the creative narrative space. From screenwriters to playwrights to novelists, the term is used to describe how to effectively map (usually in some graphical template or outline form) the key elements of the story's characters, setting, conflict, major plot points, and resolution development. In your approach to mapping content-driven experiences, you can use the spirit of both the software and narrative contexts to create a high-level structure. You can enable focused workstreams to add structural form to a larger idea that will have to be executed by cross-functional teams that won't see each other every day.

Working on this new content marketing strategy will be an ongoing process, a combination of activities that fit together nicely. In order to sustain this managed process and to scale it as a functional piece of the business, each initiative (just like every product development)

needs a structure, a purpose, and perhaps most of all, a way to measure the value created.

In short, the marketing organization (or whatever governing body
you report into) starts to operate not like a media company but *as a
media company*.

It manages a portfolio of experiential platforms that create
value for audiences. The story mapping process is a method to create the clear plan, to define the workstreams and measured tasks
that will add up to success for each individual experience within
the portfolio.

Step 1: What does success look like?

Start by doing an exercise with the editorial board that you've
identified, or at any rate a more cross-functional group than just your
immediate team. This meeting (or series of meetings) starts by
brainstorming a list of *all the things that are true* in order to consider
this content marketing initiative a success. Everything is listed here:
"We got the budget," "We integrated the right team and skills,"
"We're meeting all of our measurement goals," and even "We're winning awards for our work."

The first objection or clarifying question might be "When?" People
will want to know a timeframe for these successes. For now, resist the
urge—the timeframe will come later. Simply ask what are *all* the objectives you have, and list them out as if they have all been achieved.
You are defining the *right* map, not the one you think you can achieve
in some contained timeline.

Step 2: What are the rocks in your way?

Next, look at the list of all the things that need to be true and identify
all the known obstacles that could prevent them from happening.
Resist the urge to just state the opposite of the success statements. Be
specific about things that could derail your efforts or prevent you
from succeeding. As with Step 1, don't think of this within a timeframe for now.

Step 3: Which activities are critical?

Once you have that list of everything that needs to be true in order to envision success, as well as the rocks that are in your way, the next task is to categorize them. Go through each one and ask the team, "Which of these are showstoppers?"

What constitutes a showstopper? It's either a success statement that must be achieved in its entirety or a rock that must be circumvented completely, otherwise the initiative isn't worth doing or cannot be accomplished.

Next, determine which success statements and rocks are "testable." A testable success is when a goal has shades of gray associated with it that can (and should) be tested, or one that the team can adapt around if the success statement itself turns out not to be true. A testable rock is similar in that it may need to be avoided completely, or variations of getting around it may be showstoppers. For example:

- "We achieved budget for this initiative" is most likely a showstopper. Or, it might be testable at different budget levels, but at a certain threshold becomes a showstopper.
- "We get to use a particular brand of content management software for this platform" is most likely testable.
- "We've convinced PR to allow us to change the blog publishing process" may be either a showstopper or testable, depending on your situation.

You should end up with very few showstoppers and quite a lot of testables.

Step 4: Map your timeline

When you have your list, the next step is to plot *when* these things need to be true. The key is that you first look at all your success statements and all your rocks, especially the showstoppers, and then you ask when you will have successfully accomplished *all* of this.

Once again, you'll get pushback. People will want to exempt certain success statements and rocks. They may say things like, "Well, everything except that huge goal you have as #5 can be done within the next year." Again, resist that urge. You can always pull back. For now, the goal is to look at the totality of how you envision success and all the rocks in your path, and to set a date in the future for them all to have been resolved.

Spoiler alert: It will be a ways out.

But, once you have a date, you start with your "what success looks like" list and plot backward in time to today. Go through each success statement and plot it on your timeline (you may also start to combine them into each other). When does each need to be true? Then, do the same for the rocks. This should go quickly as they relate to one another.

A story map starts at an end point in time, then works backward to plot various value points in time.

Once you complete that (and you will almost assuredly add others to the list as you do the exercise), an interesting pattern emerges. Themes of activities, projects, and work efforts surface, but they are usually cross-functional themes. These tasks organized by theme can then be assigned to project managers who are responsible for getting them done.

The timeline, and whether a workstream is testable or a showstopper, helps to drive prioritizing the tasks. And breaking it all down for the team illustrates the flow of the activities that need to happen.

With this in mind, you can clearly communicate and inspire your teams and your C-suite, and propose a reasonable budget, timeline, and measurable strategy that will move your business forward.

If you've carefully planned your map, you should be well on your way to success. The key is to use this map as a living, breathing tool. It will change and it will evolve. Because this is a process, you can anticipate that new tests and challenges will get in your way. So, be prepared to make iterative changes based on both successes and failures.

But this first step onto the tightrope can help you deliver a team that knows exactly how to move in the same direction. A real map, if you will.

Commit to the walk

The first step was challenging. But the most challenging part will be saying "yes" to the adventure you've just designed.

One thing happens in almost every client consulting engagement I have. Once we finish the approved business case and plan, I congratulate the client. Then comes a sigh and the inevitable words: "Yeah, but now we have to go do it."

That's step two. Commit.

You commit to walking. You tackle that first big initiative. You go all in. You're not following someone else's template. You haven't dismissed those who came before you because you felt you could do as well or better. You've developed your own recipe instead of trying to improve someone else's.

The steps get easier

In the story I mentioned at the beginning of this chapter, the tightrope walker says: "The third step is the beginning. It's the complete motion forward on a new course."

Completing that first initiative or overcoming your first challenge is the beginning. That's when you start to see that things are working the way you thought they would. It's much more satisfying than looking at the next step in a templated map.

From there, the book says: "The fourth step is an affirmation. And after the fifth step—it's just walking."

The journey of a thousand miles begins with a single step and a map of where to go. That most challenging second step helps you have confidence in your journey.

You're on your way.

Note

1 Everson, J (2013) *Vigilantes of Love*, Dark Arts Books Naperville, IL, p.67

Conclusion

Forecasting the Future of Content Marketing Strategy

The only certainty about the future of any business is that it's uncertain.

Almost exactly 27 years ago, Microsoft founder Bill Gates wrote an essay called "Content Is King." In it he said that "content is where I expect much of the real money will be made on the Internet, just as it was in broadcasting."[1]

It was one of Gates's more prescient moments, because nearly three decades later it has proven to be true. The title of his essay has become a rallying cry for thousands of media and marketing strategies. A Google search on the specific phrase in quotes returns more than 1.7 million results.

But it's not the title that interests me—it's the very last line of his essay that I actually find the most visionary:

> Those who succeed will propel the Internet forward as a marketplace of ideas, experiences, and products—a marketplace of content.[2]

If we take a step back, that sentence pretty accurately describes modern marketing. Modern marketing really is just optimizing our value in a marketplace of ideas, experiences, and products—a marketplace of content.

So, when we think about the marketplace of content, what are the "big questions" that may inspire (or force) us to change our approach? Well, it comes down to what changes the ideas, experience, or products:

1 What changes the way we express our ideas?

2 What changes the types of experiences we create?

3 What changes the nature or delivery of the products our customers want?

As I said at the very beginning of this book, the perfect content marketing strategy does not exist. There is no template. Thus, once you begin, there is no finish. There is no "move on to the next thing." The most successful content marketing strategies are built with one thing in mind.

Change.

As we look up from our hard work now, we can see plenty of future disruptions that may affect the way we answer any one of those three questions. So, we obviously can't predict the future and perfectly ready ourselves for that change. But perhaps we can look back and see the "rhyming scheme" that helps us prepare for the next verse of the song.

The truth is out there... somewhere

When Bill Gates wrote his essay in 1996, one of the most popular television shows was *The X-Files*. The heroes, Fox Mulder and Dana Scully, had paranormal, supernatural, or extraterrestrial experiences that no one could explain. Their job: Search for the truth. In fact, the show's tagline was "The truth is out there."

At the heart of each week's tension were the characters' differing philosophies of science and technology. Scully's view was that no matter how "unexplainable" any phenomenon was, it could not be beyond any already applied scientific theory. Mulder, on the other hand, was quick to believe phenomena without a plausible explanation and open to using any paranormal tool even if it wasn't understood. Essentially, Mulder believed in magic and Scully thought it was all a trick.

This tension made for great television. It's also very similar to the tension that exists in the marketplace of content ideas and how it affects our approach to creating value.

On one side, you have purveyors and users of new tools and technologies for content creation who say, "It's magic." Proponents always claim that technologies have reached a point where they can replicate human work in ways that we simply cannot comprehend. Detractors worry that these tools will soon replace humans as content creators.

What is the truth? Well, the truth is out there.

For example, some say that artificial intelligence (AI)—and especially generative AI that automatically creates original content—will fundamentally change everything in content and marketing forever. Others say it has finally become useful and we must explore how it will make us more efficient. Others have actually suggested that the technology should be withdrawn because it's inherently evil.

The same holds true for what is generally known as Web3 technology. New technologies such as NFTs (non-fungible tokens) or concepts such as the metaverse have threatened to completely disrupt the practice of how ideas are expressed and transformed into digital experiences. As of the writing of this book, it's still quite unclear whether the technologies being developed for virtual worlds and cryptocurrency will become a viable opportunity for the marketplace of content.

Whether you agree or disagree with any particular take, it always comes back to our inability to predict one very particular aspect of the future. It's actually fairly straightforward to predict a fair amount of "what" will get built. You can extrapolate today's innovation and get a pretty good idea of where the actual technology is going. Now, yes, of course there are the innovations that come out of left field that surprise us. But the real trouble with predicting the future of technology is not the technology; it's how (or if) the technology will shape the future us.

We are the change, not the technology

A quote almost always misattributed to renowned media theorist Marshall McLuhan says, "We shape our tools, and thereafter our tools shape us."

This means (and it is actually the most McLuhan of ideas) that we create technology, but its existence also changes us. It then follows that the meaning of any new technology we invent comes from how it changes us.

So, for something new like artificial intelligence and content creation, we're in the former stage of that process. But the latter is coming—and that's why it's so hard to predict right now what will happen with it. So, it's no wonder that there tend to be extreme reactions to it.

Worries about inserting innovative technology into the very human creative process aren't new. After the invention of the printing press, the Dutch humanist Erasmus is said to have complained:

> To what corner of the world do they not fly, these swarm of new books? … [T]he very multitude of them is hurting scholarship because it creates a glut, and even in good things, satiety is most harmful… [Printers] fill the world with stupid, ignorant, slanderous, scandalous books, and the number of them is such that even the valuable publications lose their value.[3]

Erasmus was horrified that printing press technology would enable any no-talent hack to publish so much bad content that valuable content would be degraded as a result. Sound familiar?

The tension in the content marketplace between humans and technology has continued throughout history from the advent of mass media, the word processor, digital photography, creative software editing suites, music editing software, and computer graphics.

For example, one of my hobbies is that I am a musician. I love to play and produce music. Today, technology exists where computer programs can simulate entire choirs, enabling anyone who can type in words to create customized choral symphonies almost instantly.

For years, I've been able to transform my keyboard into a digitally sampled version of Phil Collins's drum kit and create my own versions of the classic "In the Air Tonight" solo.

So here's a question: If I compose a song using that drum kit, fill it with a sampled choir that digitally sings words I type, then I produce the song featuring cover art I made by prompting an AI engine to create an original black and white photo in the style of Ansel Adams, am I an artist or a hack?

If you said "a hack," I wonder what you would have thought almost exactly 100 years ago when musicians who would play live soundtracks to movies in theaters began to be put out of work by the newest of technologies: pre-recorded music and soundtracks on film. In 1926, more than 22,000 musicians were working in movie theater pits across the United States. They picketed, protested, and boycotted the move to "talkies" for almost 10 years. But somehow musicians and artistry survived.

But if I'm a modern artist, where do we actually draw the line? Or do we draw a line? What if the tools evolved again, and I didn't even have to type or use the piano keyboard at all. What if I could skip all the typing and playing and just ask the technology to do it for me? Would it change your answer either way?

Our wisdom will differentiate us

Regardless of which creative technology you study, the tension-filled relationship with the human creative process has always been the same:

> The fear arises that people with no experience or talent will suddenly be granted unearned abilities to create.

Which leads to the second tension:

> The fear arises that human artisans will be replaced by "hacks" or machines.

Both tensions share one thing:

> Fear.

But in every case in history, fears like this have proven unfounded. Yes, many technological innovations have removed the need for human participation in a part of the content creation process.

Digital photography removed the need for processing film in a dark room. Digital editing software removed the need for physically cutting and splicing film together. Digital word processing and imaging software removed the need for manual typesetting.

But for each successful innovation, the new technology either added a capability, made an existing activity in the creative process more efficient, or both.

So, while the fear of being replaced is almost certainly legitimate, it will only be made real if creators choose the wrong way to be changed by technology.

Put simply, today's content creator is no more or less talented or equipped to express ideas. New technologies like AI, Blockchain, the Metaverse, TikTok's algorithm, or some other new capability only change the efficiency of the activities around content.

And what do you know? There's that word again: activities. You might have guessed that I was going to come back to that.

It has always been, and will always be, our human ability to continually perform and fit together just the right activities that give us the ability to consistently produce new and creative things. We process the lessons from our experiences, combine them with our knowledge and imbue that with our own judgment to form a point of view that will create differentiated value in the marketplace of content.

Technology cannot do that. Technology only has what we give it. Therefore it can only tell us things we already believe we know.

Here's what I mean.

I prompted an artificial intelligence engine to "tell me a funny story about a marketing guy having an existential career crisis about artificial intelligence." Here's what it came up with:

> There was once a marketing guy who had a serious existential crisis due to the emergence of AI. Every day, he would go to work and worry that AI could do his job better than he ever could. He became so obsessed with his fear of being replaced that he decided to take drastic measures. One day he entered the office dressed up as an AI with a shiny metal face mask, blue LEDs flashing, and wires coming out of his ears. Everyone was so impressed by his transformation that they all applauded him and gave him a promotion. After that, the marketing guy was no longer afraid of AI and embraced its potential to help businesses grow and succeed.

You can see that the AI engine is good (quite good, actually) at constructing sentences that logically flow from one to the next. You can even see that it is pretty good at identifying the emotion of the character in the moment. But there's no uniquely emotional point of view, or even anything that resembles building a valuable, original story. It is only an interpretation of a collection of knowledge about what a story like that looks like.

Now, that's not to say that these capabilities won't be terribly helpful for us in our day-to-day world. In fact, that's the point. These technologies will shape us. We know this. Therefore, to assume that we won't elevate our own capabilities as these technologies evolve is the mistake. We evolve too.

Simply put, technology is not wise.

Wisdom is the very human quality of having the experience, knowledge, emotional intelligence, and sound judgment to help with decisions. Technology cannot currently combine these things.

Therefore, for example, technology cannot judge the wisdom of, or originate, your next differentiated white paper or ebook or marketing campaign. It won't create the most original idea for how you should approach your new podcast. It won't write the next visionary business book. It can execute something that fits the model of each of those—but it cannot originate the model itself.

But now here comes the equivocation of all equivocations. And something we all have to be willing to put at the end of all of this. It is one word. Yet!

We are the change. And while I can extrapolate and estimate how quickly the technology might get there, what I can never know is just how *we* will react. So, in my judgment, everything I've said is true—as long as I add the word "yet."

The future will be what we allow it to be

In describing the inevitability of disruptive innovation, business professor and author Clayton Christensen once shared the anecdote of a professor who dropped a pen and told his class, "I hate gravity." After a moment, he added, "But do you know what? Gravity doesn't care."[4]

The truth about all technologies is that by the time they start to shape us, they are already here. So, arguing whether it will or won't be used is a bit like asking digital photographers to put down their sim cards. We already routinely use AI to research things on Google, check our grammar, or search for the right hero image for our blog.

Now it will help us construct the written word and make images, video, and audio.

The only question that remains is how to harness it as professionals. That's where we need new wisdom.

All technology will open new doors and extend the capabilities of writers and other content creators, just as it closes doors on others. It will transform the process of written content creation in marketing. It will shape all of us.

How it will do that, though, is still up to us.

The beginning of the beginning

In 2023, Bill Gates is still right. Content is king. It is the once and future king.

I'm going to pull one last robbery, and I'll close here stealing an idea from TS White's book *The Once and Future King*, the collection of stories he wrote about King Arthur.

White ends the novel by saying:

Explicit Liber Regis Quondam Regisque Future[5]

Which is Latin for "This book ends about the once and future king."

And then the very last line of the book is:

The Beginning

The two phrases together mean that, while this book may be ending, and Arthur may have died, his ideas are just beginning to take hold. He will be back to reign again.

So I leave you as I began with you.

Your content will always be yours. But your differentiating strategy will always be in how you use it. So, as I've signed off for years, I leave you with a greeting, not a farewell.

It's your story. Tell it well.

It's just beginning.

Notes

1 Gates, B. (2001) Bill Gates' Web Site—Columns, http://web.archive.org/web/20010126005200/http:/www.microsoft.com/billgates/columns/1996essay/essay960103.asp (archived at https://perma.cc/GN7C-NBU5)
2 Ibid
3 Eisenstein, E.L. (2011) *Divine Art, Infernal Machine: The reception of printing in the West from first impressions to the sense of an ending*, Philadelphia, PA: University of Pennsylvania Press, p.25
4 Christensen, C.M. (1997) *The Innovator's Dilemma: When new technologies cause great firms to fail*, Boston, MA: Harvard Business Review Press, p.183
5 White, T.H. (2011) *The Once and Future King*, Penguin Group, New York, NY p.647

INDEX